THE

INDIAN SILVER CURRENCY

THE

INDIAN SILVER CURRENCY

AN HISTORICAL AND ECONOMIC STUDY

KARL ELLSTAETTER

TRANSLATED BY

J. LAURENCE LAUGHLIN

GYAN

Published by

Gyan Publishing House
5, Ansari Road
Daryaganj, New Delhi-110002
Phone: 011-47034999, 9811692060
E-mail: books@gyanbooks.com

Distribution Network
gyanbooks.com
India, USA, Canada, UK, Australia, France

ISBN : 978-81-212-9749-3 (PB)
First Published, 1895

2nd Impression 2023

Printed at: Gyan Press, Delhi.

THE INDIAN SILVER CURRENCY
Author: KARL ELLSTAETTER, J. LAURENCE LAUGHLIN

ECONOMIC STUDIES

OF

THE UNIVERSITY OF CHICAGO

NUMBER III.

THE INDIAN SILVER CURRENCY

AN HISTORICAL AND ECONOMIC STUDY

BY

KARL ELLSTAETTER

TRANSLATED BY

J. LAURENCE LAUGHLIN

HEAD PROFESSOR OF POLITICAL ECONOMY IN THE UNIVERSITY OF CHICAGO

1895

PREFACE.

In the discussion about standards, to no country is more attention drawn than to India; and rightly, since the fate of silver is to be decided, above all, in India. But, on this point, there exists in the Indian question considerable confusion,— as in so many parts of the currency question. Many try to veil their lack of clearness under dogmatism; and talk about axioms and elementary propositions of economics, which need no proof.

I have tried to base my conclusions principally upon the official documents which have been published at the initiative of both the English and Indian authorities, without *a priori* conceptions and in the interest of no economic or political party whatever,—for which one is unfortunately always obliged to give assurance in the discussion of the currency.

It is not consonant with the spirit of a scientific work to introduce into the field of investigation matters which cannot yet be grasped in their entirety, and upon which those closest at hand cannot yet form any judgment. The rôle of prophet is a thankless one in economics; he who wishes to give himself up to picturing the future stands quite outside of science. For this reason, I determine to investigate in this work the events only up to that point of time—to June 26, 1893—when the Indian Government closed its mints to the free coinage of silver. Should this investigation contribute somewhat to a clearer understanding of Indian affairs, I shall have accomplished my purpose.

In conclusion, permit me to express my most profound thanks to Herr Geh. Hofrat Prof. Dr. Brentano and to Herr Prof. Dr. Lotz, the directors of the economic seminar in the University of Munich. Especially to Herr Prof. Dr. Lotz do I owe the greatest thanks; he introduced me to the study of money, inspired my work, and during its progress supported me with advice and necessary scientific materials in the kindest way.

KARL ELLSTAETTER.

MUNICH, February 24, 1894.

CONTENTS.

CHAPTER I.

THE INDIAN MONETARY SYSTEM.—MOVEMENT OF THE PRECIOUS METALS.—THE USE OF THE PRECIOUS METALS.

CHAPTER II.

THE INFLUENCE OF CHANGES IN THE PRICE OF SILVER ON TRADE, AND ON THE INDUSTRIAL AND AGRICULTURAL PRODUCTION OF INDIA.

CHAPTER III.

THE FINANCIAL CONDITION OF THE EAST INDIAN GOVERNMENT.—COMPLAINTS OF ITS OFFICIALS.

CHAPTER IV.

HISTORY OF THE INDIAN SILVER CURRENCY.

APPENDIX I.

APPENDIX II.

APPENDIX III.

LITERATURE.

[EXCEPT TITLES MENTIONED IN THE TEXT.]

A. OFFICIAL DOCUMENTS.

Reports of the Royal Commission Appointed to Inquire into the Recent Changes in the Relative Values of the Precious Metals (Gold and Silver Commission), With Minutes of Evidence and Appendices. 4 vols.; London, 1886–88.

Report of the Committee Appointed to Inquire into the Indian Currency. London, 1893.

Minutes of Evidence taken before the Commission Appointed to Inquire into the Indian Currency together with an Analysis of the Evidence and Appendices. London, 1893.

Papers Relating to a Gold Currency for India. London, 1865.

Reports of the Royal Commission Appointed to Inquire into the Depression of Trade and Industry with Minutes of Evidence and Appendices. 5 Vols.; London, 1886.

Financial Statement of East India. London, 1893.

General Report of the Census of India, 1891. London, 1893.

Statement of the Trade of British India with British Possessions and Foreign Countries for the Five Years, 1885–86 to 1889–90. London, 1891.

Statement Exhibiting the Moral and Material Progress and Condition of India During the Year 1889–90. London, 1891.

Statistical Abstract Relating to British India from 1882–83 to 1891–92. London, 1893.

Statistical Abstract for the United Kingdom. Various years.

B. OTHER LITERATURE.

W. W. Hunter: The Indian Empire. London, 1882.

Ottomar Haupt: L'Histoire monétaire de notre temps. Berlin and Paris, 1886.

W. Lexis: Article, "Silber und Silberwährung," in the Handwörterbuch der Staatswissenschaften. Bd. V.

The same: "Der gegenwärtige Stand der Währungsfrage," in the Jahrbucher für Nationalökonomie und Statistik, 3. Folge; Bd. VI., p. 11.

R. Chalmers: History of Currency in the British Colonies. London, 1893.

J. Wolf: Thatsachen und Aussichten der Ostindischen Konkurrenz im Weizenhandel. Tübingen, 1886.

A. J. Macdonald: "Banking in India," in the Journal of the Institute of Bankers, 1890, p. 277.

E. Nasse: "Das Sinken der Warenpreise während der letzen 15 Jahre," in the Jahrbücher für Nationalökonomie und Statistik, Neue Folge; Bd. XVII, pp. 50 and 129.

G. Ruhland: "Aus dem Verfassungs- und Verwaltungsrecht des britisch-indischen Kaiserreichs," in the Zeitschrift für die gesammte Staatswissenschaft, 49 Jahrgang (1893), pp. 223 and 408.

J. Laurence Laughlin: "Indian Monetary History," in the Journal of Political Economy, Chicago, September, 1893, p. 593.

Guilford L. Molesworth: "Indian Currency," in the Annals of the American Academy of Political and Social Science, Philadelphia, January, 1894, p. 1.

Deutsches Handelsarchiv, published by the Imperial Department of the Interior. Various years.

The London Economist. Various years.

Journal of the Institute of Bankers. Various years.

CHAPTER I.

THE INDIAN MONETARY SYSTEM. — MOVEMENT OF THE PRECIOUS METALS.—USES OF THE PRECIOUS METALS IN THE COUNTRY.

§ 1. THE MONETARY SYSTEM.

The circulating medium of British India separates itself into three parts. The chief portion is made up (1) of the money coined by the royal Indian Government. Of far less importance than these are (2) the currency notes; and of still less importance is (3) the coin circulation of the Native States.

Let us first give attention to the coin circulation of the Native States. Quite a large number of Native States in all parts of India exercise the right of coinage, a privilege upon which they jealously insist, because it is regarded as a mark of sovereignty.[1] In each the standards are very different. The chief silver coin is the rupee with, however, many varieties in the different states. In 1835, when the present standard was introduced, there was a list of not less than 300 different kinds of rupees then existing (many of these doubtless out of use) all more or less varying from each other. The attempt made by Act IX of 1876 to bring about the acceptance of a common standard of money through the whole of India failed. For the Native States that obliged themselves not to coin for 30 years at least, and not to allow any coins like the Anglo-Indian to be struck under their authority, the act ordains that the royal Indian Government should strike coins which should be uniform in weight and fineness with those of British-India, and should have a device different from those formerly used by the respective states. Such coins should then be the legal means of payment in all India.

[1] *Report of Indian Currency Committee*, § 124 *et seq.*

Up to this time only four small states have accepted the provisions of this law, so that the much desired uniformity has not been gained. The information as to the coinage of the different Native States is not sufficient to enable us to state the amount of it. There is, however, ground for the opinion that it is not very considerable.

Hyderabad, the largest Native State, coined in 1887–8 816 gold tolas, and 15,051 silver tolas; in 1888–9 784 gold tolas, and 1,776,421 silver tolas; a tola being equal in weight to a rupee. The value of the rupee of Hyderabad, known as the Halli Sicca rupee, is about 14 per centum less than the rupee of British-India. The state of Baroda coined in 1883–4 800,000 rupees; and in 1884–5 900,000 rupees. In the three following years, however, none were coined; in 1891 the mint was provided with new machinery. The mint of Cashimir does not appear to be any longer active. Mysore and Rewah are said to have no mint; the coinage of Holkar in Indore, of Bhopal, and of Travancore are said to be unimportant.

These coins also circulate in the British provinces, especially in those lying on the borders of the respective Native States; thus the coins of Galkwar from Baroda and of Nizam from Hyderabad—both the best-known "native" rupees—are received without objection far within the British limits. Their deficiencies in value are known and a corresponding discount made.[1]

A far more important rôle than that of the coins of the Native States—in the failure of a gold medium for the indispensable wholesale exchanges—is played by the paper means of payment. Previous to 1862 the notes of the Presidency-Banks circulated, as well as the Promissory and Treasury notes issued by the Government.[2]

The "promissory notes" were drafts on the Treasury for the payment of interest on the public debt; the "treasury notes" were a kind of treasury-bills and bore interest, which varied very materially from time to time. The notes of the Presidency-

[1] *Minutes of Indian Currency Committee*, Question 2679.

[2] *Journal of the Institute of Bankers*, 1890, p. 292.

Banks were received as metallic money. For their security an amount of Government "treasury notes" equal to one-fourth of the quantity of the Bank notes in circulation must be deposited. The right to issue notes by the Presidency Banks, which had been transferred by Acts VI of 1839, III of 1840, and IX of 1843 to the banks of Bengal, Bombay, and Madras—was, according to the requirements of Act XIX of 1861, to cease from March 1st, 1862. This act (of 1861) further provided that a special "Department of Issue" should have entire charge of the issue of paper; and required also that all the precious metals, coined or in bars, which the department receives for the issue of currency notes, should be held as a reserve, with the proviso that 40,000,000 rupees—or another sum to be determined by the Governor-General—might be invested in State-paper; and that the aforesaid reserve, metallic as well as State-paper, should be kept apart always ready for the redemption of the currency notes. By the Act III of 1871 this law was amended, and it was provided that henceforth 60,000,000 Rs. of the reserve could be invested in Government paper. Act XV of 1890 raised the amount to 80,000,000 Rs. The circulation of currency notes amounted[1] on the 31st of March:

	Rx.
1871	10,437,291
1876	10,999,927
1880	12,357,727
1884	12,756,541
1885	14,576,904
1886	14,173,272
1887	13,876,836
1888	16,424,379
1889	15,737,813
1890	15,771,780
1891	25,690,449
1892	24,076,408
1893	26,401,820

[1] Appendix to the *Minutes of the Indian Currency Committee*, p. 260. The amounts in Indian Currency are expressed in the following pages partly in rupees (abbreviated to Rs.) and partly—after the manner of the Indian statistics—in an ideal unit of 10 rupees, the English pound of reckoning (abbreviated to Rx).

The extraordinary rise in 1891 was the consequence of an exceptionally great speculative shipment of silver to India in that year.[1]

The banks at that time preferred to exchange the silver which had collected in their hands for Treasury notes. They sent the silver to the Currency Department and there exchanged it for notes, so that the paper circulation increased to an excessive amount. The statement of the banks[2] at the end of 1890 shows an enormous increase in the supply of Government Treasury notes.

By far the most important rôle, moreover, in the circulation of the country is naturally played by the species of money coined by the British-Indian Government in the mints of Bombay and Calcutta. As a unit, Act XVII of 1835 introduced the silver "Company's rupee" of 180 grains Troy weight, $\frac{11}{12}$ fine, and therefore containing 165 grains (10,692 g.) fine silver. All silver brought to the mint up to June 26, 1893, was coined at seigniorage charge of 2.25 per centum. The subsidiary coinage was regulated by the Indian Coinage Act (Act XXIII) of 1870. A gold coin was also struck, the gold mohur, but only to an inconsiderable extent. Since 1835 there was coined:

	Rx.
SILVER[3]	
1835-6—1884-5	275,053,443
1885-6—1891-2	60,241,386
	335,294,829[4]
GOLD	
1835-6—1884-5	2,352,399
1885-6—1891-2	93,045
	2,445,444

The gold mohurs were receivable from 1841–1852 only in the treasuries, and are today only bought and sold.

[1] *Minutes of the Indian Currency Committee*, Questions 111–112, 266–270, 275–278, 323–325.

[2] See the Appendix to the *Minutes of Indian Currency Committee*, p. 255 *et seq.*

[3] For the figures to 1884-5, compare the *Third Report of the Commission on Depression of Trade*, p. 385 *et seq.* from 1885-6 on, the official figures given in the appendix to the *Minutes of the Indian Currency Committee*, p. 240.

[4] In this amount, the old rupees re-coined after the passage of the law of 1835 are purposely not included.

§ II. IMPORTS OF PRECIOUS METALS INTO INDIA.

	Rx. Total Import	Rx. Imports Less Exports
Amount of silver:		
1835–6—1884–5	319,183,600	263,813,338
1885–6—1891–2	80,347,557	71,372,993
	399,531,157	335,186,331
Amount of gold:		
1835–6—1884–5	137,083,018	127,888,103
1885–6—1891–2	27,971,028	23,411,682
	165,054,046[1]	151,299,785

A comparison of these figures with the amount of silver coins struck shows that the most of the silver imported into India is coined. It would be a mistake, however, to draw therefrom the conclusion—as is very frequently done—that all these coins are now in use as money. This is disclosed by the following facts: The imports of the precious metals into India, in the first place, do not depend upon the needs of the circulating medium, but quite essentially on the purchasing power of the people; that is, on the fact whether they can save more or less; and, further, whether certain exceptional events demand a very great expenditure in coin by the Government, etc. A cursory glance over the history of imports of the precious metals into India shows us this. Previous to 1855–6 the imports of the precious metals were small; and the four years following were for India exceptionally troublous. In 1857 there broke out in the north of the Empire the frightful uprising of the Sepoys, which moved the British Government to take away the control of the country from the East India Company and required unusual public expenditures. As a consequence there was imported more than exported from 1855–6 to 1859–60:

Rx. 50,362,475 silver,
" 16,091,219 gold.

The next two years were normal. In 1861, however, the American Civil War began. The Southern states of the Union could

[1] The same sources as given above for the coinage.

no longer provide the Liverpool market with cotton; and there ensued that frightful crisis for the Lancashire industries to which the English have given the fitting name of the "cotton famine."

From India, in particular, was a supply of the indispensable raw material sought for, and exceptionally high prices were paid for it. The value of the exports of cotton from India rose from Rx. 4.64 millions (1859–60) to Rx. 27.57 millions (1865–6). Consequently the imports of the precious metals increased very greatly:

	Excess Imports over Exports
Silver	
1860–1	Rx. 5,328,009
1865–6	" 18,668,673
Gold	
1860–1	" 4,232,569
1865–6	" 5,724,476

The next years were quieter. In consequence of divers bad harvests, as well as of the panic in India succeeding the cotton famine, a considerable decrease in the imports of the precious metals ensued. In 1870–1 only Rx. 941,931 of silver was imported in excess of exports.

After 1870 began that fall in the price of silver, the chief causes of which some people seek for in the increased production of silver, and others in the continued withdrawal of silver from the rôle of a European metallic standard.

However, before the fall in the price of silver could exercise its full influence on India, a frightful catastrophe befell the country.[1]

In 1875 the monsoon did not appear in Mysore; a great drought and a fatally bad harvest was the result. In the summer of 1876 this was repeated throughout the whole Deccan. In the autumn of the same year, the northeast monsoon did not appear in the southeast of the Presidency of Madras; the harvest failed over an extensive region; and, since the harvest of 1875 had been small, famine prices were soon demanded everywhere. In addition the drought in 1877 had reached the north; the provinces of the northwest, Punjab, Rájputána, and the Central pro-

[1] Hunter, *The Indian Empire*, p. 429.

vinces suffered dreadfully. Until 1879 the famine continued; then came the cholera, which, especially in the limits of Madras, swept off hundreds and hundreds of thousands. In the years 1877 and 1878, according to the estimate of the "Famine Commission," the population was reduced by 5.25 millions. The result of this unexampled catastrophe was, of course, a serious decrease in the purchasing power of the people and consequently of the imports of the precious metals. In 1875–6 the net amount of silver imports was Rx. 1,555,355; and of gold, Rx. 1,545,131. Both the next years show a marked importation of silver, because the Government—in order to counteract the distress—sent large sums to India. Yet the net importation of gold fell seriously, amounting in

1876–7 to Rx. 207,349
1877–8 " " 468,129

and in 1878–9 the exports exceeded the imports by Rx. 896,173.

After the distress was removed, the purchasing power of the Indian people again increased. The balance of trade was never before so favorable. The imports of the precious metals increased very markedly. In the years 1880–1 to 1884–5 the average yearly excess of imports over exports of silver amounted to Rx. 6,080,727, and of gold to Rx. 4,712,899; in 1885–6 to 1889–90 of silver to Rx. 9,635,135, and of gold to Rx. 3,072,343. Strange to say, we find especially large imports of the precious metals in 1890–1. The American coinage law raised the price of silver, which for a time (May 1889) had fallen below 42 pence, to 54½d. (August 1890) The average price for 1890 was $47\frac{11}{16}$d. as compared with $42\frac{1}{16}$d. for the year 1889. In connection with this rise in the price of silver there followed a movement of the net imports of silver up to Rx. 14,175,136. It is generally stated that this import in great part originated with speculators; and the bank statements prove this. (Cf. p. 4.) A report of the imperial German Consul-General[1] at Calcutta says on this point: "While the high prices of silver existed, it was profitable to bring silver to India. The quantity of silver

[1] *Deutsches Handelsarchiv*, 1891, vol. ii. p. 619.

imported in the year 1890–1 far exceeded the needs of trade, and this silver brought into India for the purposes of speculation is not therefore to be found in circulation, but rests in the bank like capital waiting for investment." According to this, as it appears, the Indian speculators in silver were waiting for a higher rise in the price of silver, because in no other way can the phenomenon be explained. There apparently existed among the people no need for this quantity of silver; they rather profited by the opportunity after so long a time to be able to acquire gold at a low rate; and the consequence was an excess of imports of gold over exports of Rx. 5,636,172. The reaction soon followed.

When, in spite of the Sherman bill, the price of silver in 1891 again dropped, and the speculators beheld themselves cheated in their expectations, the speculative shipments of silver again ceased; but, in consequence of the unusually favorable balance of trade (exports of goods amounted to Rx. 108,173,592 as against imports of Rx. 69,432,383) the excess of silver imported rose to the height of Rx. 9,022,184. The year 1892 brought a very precipitate fall in the price of silver, the quotation in the London bourse falling below 38d. That was an opportunity for the Indians, which had never before occurred, to get silver in exchange for gold; never before could one buy so much silver with one's gold. Hence the Indian statistics for 1892–3 show the phenomenon, to that time unheard of (except the unusual case of the famine of 1878–9 in which, however, the excess of exports over imports of gold was only Rx. 896,173) of an excess of exports over imports of gold of Rx. 2,812,683. At the same time the imports of silver, of course, rose, since the balance of trade continued to remain favorable; although the height of the net imports of silver in the year 1890–1, namely Rx. 12,863,569, was not reached.

§ III. THE USE OF THE PRECIOUS METALS IN INDIA.

From what has been said in the previous section it appears that the imports of silver into India depend upon anything rather than upon the needs of the country's circulating medium. We found, to be sure, that almost all the imported silver is coined; but that, however, is far from saying that these silver coins remain in circulation. In many cases the coining appears to have value to the native only in that, when he has a rupee, he knows exactly how much of the commodity silver he has. All experts on Indian conditions agree on these points.

Sir David Barbour, in his estimate of June 21, 1892, states the existing circulation of rupees to be Rx. 115,000,000.[1] According to other very careful computations, it is Rx. 120,000,000; while the figure stated by Ottomar Haupt, of Rx. 180,000,000, is probably too high. It should not, however, escape attention that the coined rupees are shipped again to a very considerable amount out of the country;[2] for the Indian rupee supplies the medium of exchange for East Africa, Ceylon, and the countries on the Persian Gulf. By far the greatest part of the exports of silver from India go to the countries mentioned;[3] while to Europe a very small amount of silver, and to America and Australia absolutely none, is exported. An exact determination of the amount of rupees to be found in actual circulation in India is absolutely impossible, because, as has been already expounded, great quantities of silver in the form of coins are hoarded, and it is not easy to draw the line between the hoarded rupees and those which might again come into circulation.

It has long been recognized that the hoards in India were exceedingly large, and yet, until recently it was impossible to get authentic information thereon. The experts heard before the various English commissions have expressed themselves wholly in generalities. It was hence very commendable in Sir David Barbour that, in 1886, he began exact investigations on this

[1] Appendix to *Minutes of Indian Currency Committee*, p. 147. Cf. also p. 273.

[2] For the regions under the control of Germany, German rupees are now struck.

[3] According to the statements of the *Statistical Abstract* these are:

	To Ceylon	To Africa	To Arabia and Persia
1889–90	Rx. 602,221	Rx. 217,564	Rx. 236,366
1890–91	" 650,750	" 188,930	" 142,038
1891–92	" 769,150	" 51,333	" 281,532

highly important matter, the results of which he laid before the Royal Gold and Silver Commission.[1]

During his eight years of activity as Magistrate and Collector (the highest administrative officer of a district) in the interior of the Indian Empire, in daily contact with the native population, this eminent financier had a rich opportunity to get exact information on the conditions in question.

In the first place, it is true of both metals that they are changed into ornaments in extraordinary quantities. Even the "globe-trotter" hurrying through the country with the speed of an express-train is impressed with the way in which the natives are loaded with the precious metals. One cannot take up a book of travels on India in which the author does not give expression to his amazement on this point. Just as soon as the Indian has saved anything, he buys himself an ornament, the rich, one of gold, the less wealthy, one of silver.

So far as gold is concerned, it is the article of an extensive trade in India. The gold-traders obtain their gold in Calcutta or Bombay, and sell it in small quantities to the people who desire it. According to the assurances of the experts, when a banker, or gold-trader, does business with an Indian, he is always ready to take gold in payment, because he knows its market price, and can almost always carve out a profit. Gold mostly circulates in the form of sovereigns, or of bars weighing 10 ounces, $\frac{998}{1000}$ fine. Still, one cannot speak of a gold circulation in the ordinary sense of the word: it is only an article of trade.

A relatively small quantity of gold is directly lost. This holds true, for example, of the cloths worked with gold, which frequently contain 10 per centum of gold. The gold can be recovered, it is true, by burning the material; but it is said not to happen frequently.

We learn from Delhi of a remarkable way of using gold.[2] In the native ceremonial, if one wishes to give a visitor a sign for his departure, he gives him a "pledge," *i. e.* a little ornament,

[1] *First Report*, Questions 1095 *et seq.*; as well as Appendix V, A–D.

[2] *First Report of Gold and Silver Commission*, Question 1131.

which contains a small quantity of gold. Although the quantity of the precious metal contained in it is too diminutive to permit the receiver to convert it into value, yet—what is undoubtedly only a remotely approximate estimate—about £100 are daily used in Delhi for "pledges" for guests.

A great quantity of gold escapes into the treasuries of the Rajahs. Mr. Barbour laid before the Gold and Silver Commission, for example, a detailed description of the stored-up wealth of the Maharajah of Burdwan. Seven great vaults are filled with gold, silver, and precious stones, all worked up into dishes, table-equipment, articles for religious ceremony, and even stools and tables; besides, there are heaps of coins and uncoined metals. These vaults are under the charge of the Ranee, although even she may enter them only in the company of the Rajah. An extract from a report of a post-office official, who is regarded as especially trustworthy, which was published at the same time, is interesting.[1] He ascertained from a native prince that he annually caused £40–45,000 of gold to be bought in Bombay and Calcutta and sent with the greatest secrecy to his residence, to be stored there. At the conclusion he says: "If inquiry be made, it will most probably be found that this is really the case; but the mischief which such an inquiry will cause by exciting distrust and suspicion of the real intentions of the government will be serious, and should not, I think, be risked without urgent reasons, and then only with great caution." It is seen from this what strong reason there is for not possessing as yet any authentic, official information as to the hoards.

The stored-up treasures are treated like a gallery of ancestors; they are not drawn upon, so long as any other shift is possible, and it is regarded as a matter of family honor not to touch them. Thus, Mr. Barbour tells of a prince who, although at his death he left £4,000,000—a great part of it in precious metals—in the year 1877 willingly allowed £500,000 to be advanced by the government rather than draw upon the family treasure.

The quantities of the precious metals, likewise, which are col-

[1] *First Report of Gold and Silver Commission*, p. 323.

lected in the temples are very considerable. These are quite as unlikely to be touched as those in the vaults of the princes.

The answer to the question, What is done with the silver? is much more difficult. For, in this, one does not have to do with a relatively small number of rich people, but with the millions on millions who make up the mass of the Indian population. In order to obtain at least a foundation for this matter, E. J. Sinkinson, Accountant General of the Punjab, at the suggestion of Mr. Barbour, in 1886 tried to ascertain how much silver was absorbed by the mountain population of Simla. The conditions existing here are exceedingly favorable for an investigation of this sort. It is one of the smallest districts of all India, containing in its limits of 102 English square miles 44,642 inhabitants.[1] It is wholly shut in by mountains. Owing to the presence of a great number of Europeans during the summer—Simla is, as is well known, the residence of the Central Government of the Indian Empire in summer—much money is expended there which does not flow back to the plains. Mr. Sinkinson's report says:[2]

"The silver remittances from treasuries in the plains to Simla and Kasanli (a sub-treasury of Simla) during the last 25 years have been as follows:

1861–1886, Total, Rs. 66,402,850.

"The amount of silver brought to Simla, otherwise than in remittances on account of government, may be neglected. European and native bankers and traders replenish their resources when necessary by currency notes which the Simla treasury is always prepared to cash.

"The amount of silver brought by visitors is insignificant. Remittances of coin to the plains are never made, either by the Government, or bankers, or merchants. Remittances are made either by currency notes or by treasury bills on Bombay, Calcutta, Umballa, Lahore and Delhi, which the treasury is always prepared to grant.

[1] *Census Report of 1891*, p. 19.

[2] *First Report of Gold and Silver Commission*, Appendix V, A.

"The currency notes supplied to the Simla treasury during the last three years have been:

	Rs.
1883-4 - - - - - -	834,000
1884-5 - - - - - - -	1,345,000
1885-6 - - - - - -	1,541,000

"The treasury bills issued by Simla treasury during the last three years have been:

	Rs.
1883-4 - - - - - -	780,700
1884-5 - - - - - - -	1,475,400
1885-6 - - - - - -	1,969,500

"The aggregate of these notes and bills represent remittances on account of banking, trading, etc., made to the plains.

"A portion of the silver sent to Simla by government eventually returns to the plains. The Simla market is supplied with cattle, grain, and miscellaneous supplies largely from the plains.

"A large portion of these supplies is brought by intinerant peddlers, who take back cash with them for fresh purchases in the villages where currency notes would not be accepted. I have not been able to procure any satisfactory information from the Simla octroi returns, as it is impossible to make any accurate distribution of the amount of business done by large dealers, who would not remit cash, and by intinerant traders with small capital, who take back cash. Most of the grain supply of Simla is brought up by Zamindars from Ludhiana and Ferozepore, who take back coin. The retail grain dealers are mostly Hosiarpore and Kaugra men, who come to Simla for the season, and are believed to take back their profits in coin. The cost of carriage of supplies is also considerable, and nearly all of it is taken back in cash. So are the savings of carpenters, masons, and domestic servants from the plains. Looking to the class of people who take back coin, and to the fact that it is certainly not taken in large quantities at a time, I do not think that it can exceed one-third of the amount sent to Simla by the Government, or about Rs. 1,100,000 yearly. Applying this to the results of the past six years, it may be taken that the present annual absorption of silver by the hill population is about Rs. 2,200,000 a year.

AMOUNT OF SILVER SENT TO SIMLA.

	Rs.
1880–1	3,293,000
1881–2	3,200,000
1882–3	3,288,000
1883–4	4,115,000
1884–5	3,148,000
1885–6	2,468,000
	3) 19,512,000
	6,504,000
	6) 13,008,000
	2,168,000

This result is the more curious when it is considered how sparse the hill population is, and that the Thibet traders ordinarily take back grain and not silver. I think that the hill population is acquiring wealth rapidly. It is certain that many of the hill rajahs, notably those of Rampore, Busahir, and Bilaspore, have accumulated large stores of silver; and it cannot have escaped observation how the fact of growing wealth is reflected in the amount of silver and gold ornaments now worn by hill women. It is nearly 10 years since I first came to Simla, and the change in this respect in that period is sufficiently striking."

Of the silver thus absorbed, it is certain that only a small part remains in circulation; but one may not generalize from the example of the mountain people without wider knowledge, for there are probably few places in India where the people have such favorable chances for large earnings as at the summer residence of the viceroy.

In regard to the amount of the silver circulation, the fact should not escape attention that probably in no country of the world are there so many money-lenders, or, as the English somewhat euphemistically call them, bankers, as in India. Sir Richard Temple estimates their number at 250,000, or nearly $\frac{1}{1000}$ of the population.[1] They, of course, always possess con-

[1] *Journal of the Institute of Bankers*, 1890, p. 300. This figure cannot be an over-estimate, for according to the last enumeration the number of money-lenders and their dependents amounted to 1,128,288. Under this, however, are included pawn-lenders, who in the country appear to do a "banking" business frequently in the form of making advances on ornaments.—*Census Report*, p. 107.

siderable ready money. Still, the amount of this should not be overestimated; for a great part of the business is so conducted that the banker (almost every village has one) advances corn in kind to the farmer at the planting-season, and has it paid back to him again after the harvest with usurious interest.

On the question of the distribution of the precious metals a letter from a former Inspector-General of Police in Punjab, published in the London *Economist*,[1] is interesting. This official had prepared an approximate estimate of the amount of gold and silver which was stolen for three years in the Punjab, and arrived at a sum of about Rx. 60,000 for each metal. While this sum of silver, however, was spread over the whole land, gold was stolen chiefly in only those districts which contain the larger cities, such as Delhi, Amritsur, Peshawur, Multan.

Is there no prospect that some of the enormous masses of the precious metals which have disappeared in India in the course of thousands of years, may again come to light? Only in case the balance of payments of the country should disclose a permanent indebtedness. At the time of a general famine the imports of gold, to be sure, diminish—nay, are even converted into an export of gold; yet, this is naturally only a passing phenomenon. At the close of the seventies, as already mentioned, a frightful famine raged in the most dissimilar parts of the mighty empire; at that time the gold movement of the country amounted in Rx. to:

	Imports of Gold	Exports of Gold	Excess
1875–76	1,836,381	291,250	1,545,131
1876–77	1,443,711	1,236,362	207,349
1877–78	1,578,927	1,110,798	468,129
1878–79	1,463,050	2,359,223	— 896,173 !
1879–80	2,050,393	299,889	1,750,504
Average........	1,674,492	1,059,504	614,988

At other times the excess of gold imports is about 8 to 10

[1] No. 2582 (February 18th, 1893), p. 205.

times as large as during these years of famine. The year 1892–3, however, presents a very marked exception, such as the Indian statistics had never before recorded. The imports of gold amounted to Rx. 1,781,789, the exports on the other hand to Rx. 4,594,472; hence excess of exports was Rx. 2,812,683. These facts permit no other explanation than that the natives, because of the strikingly low quotations of silver—or, as seen from their standpoint, because of the strikingly high quotations of gold,—were induced to exchange their gold for an extraordinarily large amount of silver.

The influence of a famine makes itself felt in silver in that more ornaments, old silver coins, etc., are sent in to the mint. Although the amount of ornaments so coined is quite small in ordinary years, yet from 1877 to 1880 Rx. 4,500,000 of silver ornaments came to the mints at Bombay and Calcutta. The imports of silver did not diminish in these years, because the Government sent large amounts of silver to India in order to institute measures of relief with the necessary energy.

Very gradually a few enlightened people are beginning to find it profitable to invest their savings, after, so to speak, a more European fashion, instead of buying ornaments with them, or burying precious metals in the earth; thus there is already said to be in the hands of the natives a very considerable part of the stock of the cotton mills in the presidency of Bombay.

But the savings banks also are becoming more and more naturalized. The deposits[1] amounted to:

Year	Total Deposits Rx.	Average Deposit Rx.
1884–85	4,687,082	19
1885–86	5,081,183	19
1886–87	5,795,249	20
1887–88	6,675,571	20
1888–89	7,622,544	20
1889–90	7,531,868	18
1890–91	8,062,241	17
1891–92	8,886,372	17

[1] *Financial Statement*, 1893–4, p. 70.

As can be inferred from the decrease in the average amount of the single deposits, people of small means are beginning to make use of the savings banks. The same phenomenon is evidenced by the Postal savings banks. The statistical abstract gives the following figures:[1]

	Number of Native Depositors	Deposits of Natives Rx.	Average Deposit Rx.
1887–88	227,865	4,223,252	185
1888–89	273,696	5,008,203	183
1889–90	315,121	5,047,546	160
1890–91	362,368	5,570,820	154
1891–92	411,107	6,170,175	150

For the year 1889–90, it was reported:

"The figures of the last two years seem to show that the savings bank system is beginning to reach the agricultural population in the districts. The number of depositors who are farmers is almost twice as great as it was two years ago; and the increase of this class of depositors in 1889–90 was 42.62, a far higher percentage of increase than in the depositors of any other class."

Yet, probably all this above-mentioned tendency cannot easily eradicate hoarding from the habits of the people; it is a usage much too deeply rooted. For centuries have the unwarlike Hindoos been accustomed to be robbed of their property by the bold Mahrattas, often too by robbers; too frequently had the enemy invaded the country and despoiled it of what they could find. In addition to this, an Asiatic ruler seldom had any other purpose than to fill his own purse as quickly as possible with the wealth of his subjects. Consequently, nothing was more natural than that the native, never sure of his possessions for an hour, should acquire the habit of investing his money in objects which could be easily hidden, such as precious metals and jewels. Consideration, moreover, must be given to the wife and children. Even if a man knows that he is acting more wisely when he invests his savings in securities, in savings banks, etc., still after

[1] *Statement on Moral and Material Progress of India*, p. 180.

his death his widow would be at a loss, because an uninstructed Hindoo woman would not know what to do with the documents.

It was an advantage for Europe and America that the native Indians persisted in their ancient customs. If there were no export of silver from Europe to India, the price of silver must have fallen in a fashion radically different from that which has so far taken place; for the largest and most regular customer would have been taken away. This, however, has not always been so regarded. In the fifties and sixties when, in consequence of the discoveries of gold in California and Australia, gold was almost the only metal coined in the countries of Europe having a double-standard, and when silver on the other hand flowed away to India, which took large amounts because of the Sepoy Rebellion and the "cotton famine," a very real solicitude was widely entertained. A report of the Chamber of Commerce at Bombay to the viceroy, Sir John Lawrence, in the year 1864,[1] runs:

"9. That India alone, therefore, has consumed during the last six years on an average 15 per cent., and last year nearly 50 per cent., more silver than the world annually produces.

"11. That great scarcity and enhancement in the value of silver must inevitably ensue from this excessive disproportion between demand and supply.

"12. That the inevitable decrease in the amount of our currency, therefore, just at a time when the amount of commodities to be circulated has so enormously increased, and a consequent violent derangement of prices, cannot fail to be most disastrous to India.

"13. That the continued drain of silver for India must derange, if not eventually destroy, the silver currency of all other nations.

"14. That it is the interest of the world, as well as of India, to check the exhaustive drain of silver, by the introduction of gold into our currency."

If gold were to be substituted for the word "silver" in this interesting extract, it might be thought we were listening to a

[1] *Papers Relating to a Gold Currency for India*, London, 1865, pp. 7 *et seq.*

Cassandra-like warning, such as are now the order of the day in regard to the exports of gold to India. The fear is now often expressed that the continued movement of gold to India must bring confusion, if not eventual destruction, to the gold standard of all other nations. It remains to wait and see whether this fear is better founded than that entertained in regard to the silver standard thirty years ago by the first Chamber of Commerce of the Indian Empire. The production of gold has until now sufficed to supply the needs of the civilized world as well as of India. And even if, in the further development of the latest monetary reform, a limping gold standard should be established in India, gold would then, as always before, be required on the whole only for foreign trade and the inland hoards; a very small amount would be required for the inland medium of exchange, because gold coins, in by far the greatest number of Indian exchanges, represent far too great a value. That the Indian demand for silver, even after the cessation of the free coinage of silver, will cease abruptly, is scarcely to be supposed; for it is precisely the vast masses of people, who have hoarded their little savings in the form of silver from the earliest times; and it is impossible for them to transfer these into gold, because for them gold is so dear as to be out of reach. There is yet a further consideration: according to the estimate of Mr. Barbour, in a population of 287 millions and an active circulation of 1150 millions of rupees, there are only four rupees per capita, a very extraordinarily small sum, even in comparison with the poorest countries of Europe. This is explicable only on the ground that the vast mass of the Indian population are yet living wholly in a state of barter. This extends, as the last census reports emphasize, over the entire country population, and the Indian agricultural population, to the number of 260 millions, make up the enormous majority of the inhabitants. The "village community," which is spread over all India, forms a world in itself, and the village artisans, among whom, strangely enough, the jeweler belongs, are paid by barter, either by the conveyance of a piece of land, or by a share of the harvest. But, in more recent times, elements have joined this microcosm, which are not essentially its own; and the small dealers, the grain-traders, etc., form the means of communication with the outside world. Inasmuch as these trade from village to village, they no longer depend upon barter, but use money in their transactions. With the development of trade these dealers penetrate deeper and deeper into the interior of the country, and thus conduce to the extension of the monetary régime. The more this is widened, the greater will undoubtedly be the demand for a metallic medium of exchange in India. Then, since the hoards, as we said above, are for the greater part composed of coined rupees, an increased demand for the circulating medium will probably be first supplied from these;[1] so much the more, since recently the native obtains for the coined rupee more silver than the weight of the silver in the rupee. If these coins, coming out of the hoards into free circulation, should be replaced by hoards of uncoined silver, a larger import of silver would thereby be occasioned. In the remoter future, however, should the natives perceive that uncoined stores of silver—in consequence of the cessation of the free coinage of silver—are exchanged only at a loss, then coined silver would be again preferred for hoarding purposes, that is for the laying up of an "honest penny." Then the Government which has reserved to itself the right to coin the silver in case of need, would be obliged, in order to satisfy an increasing demand for the circulation, to coin a larger amount of silver, and to import it into India for this purpose.

From all these considerations it can scarcely be claimed—as has so often been done either by the advocates of the gold standard, or by the bimetallists, in the first shock on the cessation of Indian coinage—that the rôle of silver has been played to the last act; since, so long as the vast masses of people in eastern Asia hold fast to silver, it is not to be supposed that it has lost its character as a money metal.

[1] Mr. Goschen called attention to this possibility in the House of Commons, December 13, 1893.

CHAPTER II.

THE INFLUENCE OF CHANGES IN THE PRICE OF SILVER ON TRADE, AND ON THE INDUSTRIAL AND AGRICULTURAL PRODUCTION OF INDIA.

§ I. FLUCTUATIONS OF THE EXCHANGES.

Up to the cessation of the free coinage of silver in India—ordained in 1893—complaint was especially made of two evils which made themselves felt in the trade with countries having a gold standard: (1) the violent fluctuations in the rate of exchange, and (2) the depreciation of silver. Each of these must be sharply distinguished from the other. First, we shall treat of the effect of the continual fluctuations of the rupee on the foreign trade of India. Upon the importance of it opinions are divided: as it is, very many experts assure us that the representations on this subject are very much exaggerated. Almost all the experts called before the Gold and Silver Commission, as well as before the Herschell Committee, admit that in normal times those engaged in trade can protect themselves against the fluctuations in the rate of exchange which take place between the reception of the order and the delivery of the goods ordered. The Indian importer first simply transmits by telegraph to his European house the orders which come to him from the home merchant. Only on a confirmed order is work begun; consignees are unwilling to keep warehouses full of goods ready for sale on account of the great risk. On the completion of the order, the importing house [in India] can protect itself against the fluctuations of exchange by buying of a banker on the spot gold-values to the amount of the rupees which he is to receive on the delivery of the goods from the one who gave the order. Of course, the banker does not undertake this risk for nothing;

still the premium may be small, because there exists a great market for bills to and from India, as well as for Government bills. Only in times of very violent fluctuations are the bankers said to refuse to buy or sell bills, at longer time than the trade with India demands, to customers to whom they do not have to pay especial attention.

In other ways, too, just such violent fluctuations of the exchanges are undesirable for trade; in such times the Indian holds back his orders entirely, and it is credible that—as is pretty generally asserted—in periods of violent fluctuations in the rate of exchange, trade for a time comes to a complete standstill.

The importer gets into a bad situation when, by some unfortunate circumstance such as cannot be avoided in the trade with so distant a land as India, the delivery of the goods is delayed and meanwhile the rate of exchange has fallen; in such a case it is said to happen frequently that the Indian dealer refuses to fulfill his contract, and the importing house has to carry the loss. In such cases a compromise is generally made at a lower price, and the sums thus lost are said to be not inconsiderable.[1]

To this point have we gone in picturing the processes by which the Indian importer finds it possible, in normal times during the existence of a silver standard, to give orders on the basis of gold values to the European manufacturer. If, however, a European manufacturer was found ready to take orders on the basis of the rupee-standard, then the protection from the exchanges was, of course, the concern of the manufacturer.

To what extent the firms engaged in the Indo-European trade protect themselves against fluctuations in the rate of exchange by time-contracts in bar-silver, I could not learn. A time-contract in silver would have exactly the same result as a transaction in long-time bills of exchange; because the rate of exchange on India, up to the cessation of the free coinage of silver, followed exactly the fluctuations of price in the silver market. Let us suppose a case in which the protection against

[1] *Gold and Silver Commission*, Question 2264.

the exchanges is the concern of the European manufacturer. Should a Manchester cotton spinner, for example, accept an order in January 1892, for cotton yarn to be delivered at Bombay, payable on July 1 in rupees, he would be entirely protected against any influence arising from fluctuations in the rate of exchange if he should sell a corresponding amount of bar-silver for the last of June 1892, in blanco, at the quotation of the day on the London Exchange. If the rate of exchange falls below this, then he loses on his goods-contract, although he gains by the speculation in the fall of silver; if the rate of exchange rises, then he loses on silver, but gets a profit on the delivery of the goods. How far this method, however, has come into use as a protection against the exchanges, I could not, as already mentioned, learn.

The reverse of these operations, as when the importer into India undertakes to cover any loss from exchange, of course, always take place in the export trade; and the exporter from India, or the importer into England, can always protect himself by time-dealings in bills [*Devisen*] or in bar-silver, at the last moment on the departure of the ship on which the goods bought or sold are freighted.

In the computations the cost of insurance against loss by exchanges is as exactly worked out as the cost of marine insurance.

The condition of the Indian importer occasionally assumes an unpleasant phase, if he is obliged to wait until he receives the money from his customers. In recent years, as a rule, he lost nothing, for the price of silver steadily fell, and it was favorable to him; he lost nothing, nay he could even gain a profit by the rise in the prices of his goods caused by a decline in the rate of exchange. Only in 1890 things went badly; the rate of exchange then rose high; the prices of European goods correspondingly fell, and the dealers who had to sell the imported goods, had to meet the loss. The native merchants of Kurrachee, an exceedingly flourishing seaport at the mouth of the Indus, because the firms engaged in the importation of cotton goods lost heavily in 1890 by the sudden rise of exchange, and the exporters of grain also had lost heavily by the fall in 1891, resolved, as a consequence, in 1892 to buy no more European goods.[1]

The former had obtained the goods when the exchanges were low, and when the prices of goods consequently were high; then when the rate of exchange rose and as a result the prices of cotton goods fell, they had to face the danger of losing, and they tried to raise prices by holding back their goods. The speculation miscarried, because large quantities of goods came from Bombay, so that prices could not be kept up.

The sudden rise of exchange in 1890 had another and significant influence on the trade of Kurrachee.[2] A great wool trade is carried on in this city; the wool is brought down the Indus from Afghanistan and there sold to dealers who cleanse and ship it. As a result of the rise in the rate of exchange in 1890 the price of wool dropped very seriously; then the Afghans were told that it was the rupee that was at fault. The honest sons of the mountain believed that the Government had done something [or other] wrong to the rupee. They wrote to Afghanistan not to send any goods until the sircar or Government should leave the rupee alone. By this means trade was very sensibly injured, but because the rise of exchange was only temporary, it soon resumed its normal course again.

The judgment as to the operation of the fluctuations of exchange during the time of the free coinage of silver which the Herschell Committee states in section 25 of its report is important on this point: "It is said that legitimate trade is replaced by mere speculation and gambling. There seems to be a common agreement amongst those who differ in their views upon almost all other points, that trade is seriously harassed by these fluctuations, though the estimates do not all agree as to the character and the extent of the inconvenience arising from this cause. It does not appear to be certain, even in the view of

[1] *Minutes of the Indian Currency Committee*, Questions 311 *et seq.*, and also p. 154.

[2] *Ibid.*, Question 312.

those who are most strongly sensible of the mischievous effects of fluctuations of exchange, that the volume of trade over a series of years has been diminished from this cause, though there seems a common agreement that any sudden or violent fluctuation almost paralyzes business for a time. It is to be observed that it is not so much the fall of exchange which is complained of, as the fluctuations, whether in one direction or the other. Some of those who admit the mischief to trade of exchange fluctuations allege that the extent of the mischief is not serious, since provision can be largely made against the effects of these fluctuations through the medium of banks, but it is clear that the trades cannot completely safeguard themselves in this way, and that such security as they obtain in this respect must be paid for. It must be remembered that before the fall in the price of silver began, and the fluctuations in the rate of exchange dependent upon it, the rates of exchange varied very considerably during particular years, though, no doubt, the fluctuations have been much more frequent and considerable since that time.

"Upon the whole it cannot be doubted it would be well if commerce were free from the inconveniences of fluctuations which arise from a change in the relation between the standard of value in India and in countries with which her commerce is transacted. It must not be assumed that the adoption of the same standard for the United Kingdom and India would remove all the disquieting causes of the disturbance of trade of which complaint is made. If the commodity which lies behind the exchange transaction is one that continues to fall in relation to gold, the risk which arises from bargains in a falling market will still be present. The liability of the standard of the one country to fall, in relation to the other, causes, however, an additional risk, and consequently increased disturbance to trade."

§ II. EFFECTS OF THE FALL IN THE VALUE OF SILVER.

A. EFFECT ON PRICES.

Much more important, however, is the question, how the fall in the price of silver *per se* affected not only trade, but the industrial and agricultural production of India. The question is the more difficult to answer, because the period, in which the relation between gold and silver changed so seriously, witnessed a complete revolution in the conditions of trade in the country. In 1869 the Suez Canal was opened, and thereby eastern Asia was first brought very near to Europe. Hand in hand with this came an increasing tendency to replace sailing vessels by steamships.

Year	Steamships				Total	
	Entering		Clearing			
	Number	Tonnage	Number	Tonnage	Number	Tonnage
1871-72..........	212	234,782	208	229,416	420	464,198
1880-81..........	686	1,018,103	773	1,115,769	1459	2,133,872
1882-83..........	711	1,152,440	934	1,433,480	1645	2,585,920
1891-92..........	1043	2,019,482	1268	2,412,341	2311	4,431,824
			Ships of All Kinds.			
1882-83..........	5864	3,538,878	5851	3,533,006	11,715	7,071,844
1891-92..........	5686	4,308,375	5472	4,282,276	11,158	8,590,651

Not less important is the increase of railways. On December 31, 1870, there were in operation 4475 English miles. In 1880 there were already 9308; in 1890, 16,404, and on March 31, 1893, 18,042 miles. The annual average in English miles put into operation in 1871–1880 was 453.3; in 1881–1890, 709.6; from January 1, 1891, to March 31, 1893, 728. The increase is, therefore, not only absolutely very large, but it is also an extraordinary progressive rise. As a matter of course a revolution is thereby created in the domestic trade of the Indian penisula, similar to that caused by the opening of the Suez Canal in the trade with Europe.

Parallel to it goes a considerable reduction in the rates of freight by land and water. In a publication appearing shortly before his death, *Das Sinken der Warenpreise während der Letzten fünfzehn Yahre*—the most valuable investigation on Indian economics which I have met with in German literature,—Nasse gives the following figures from the *Statement of the Trade of British India*, 1887:

RATES OF FREIGHT FOR RICE AND WHEAT FROM CALCUTTA TO LONDON BY STEAMSHIP VIA THE CANAL.

Period	Amount							Increase or decrease of freight-rate in each year
	£	s.	d.		£	s.	d.	Per Cent.
December 13, 1870	2	15	0	to	3	5	0	
" 5, 1871	3	10	0	"	3	12	6	+ 18.75
" 5, 1872	3	10	0					— 1.75
" 11, 1873	3	0	0					— 14.29
" 3, 1874	1	15	0					— 41.66
" 9, 1875	2	8	9	"	2	11	3	+ 67.86
" 7, 1876	3	17	6	"	4	0	0	+ 34.04
" 13, 1877	1	10	0	"	1	15	0	— 58.73
" 12, 1878	1	0	0	"	1	5	0	— 30.77
" 4, 1879	3	10	0	"	3	15	0	+ 222.22
" 7, 1880	2	16	3	"	2	18	9	— 20.69
" 10, 1881	3	0	0	"	3	2	6	+ 6.52
" 4, 1882	1	13	9	"	1	16	3	— 42.85
" 3, 1883	1	5	0	"	1	7	6	— 25.00
" 8, 1884	1	5	0					— 4.76
" 14, 1885	1	7	6	"	1	10	0	+ 15.00

The decrease in the rates of freight since 1870, therefore, amounts to 52.08 per centum. The author adds the following remarks: "At present the freight from Calcutta to London on wheat costs 24 per centum, and that on rice 20 per centum, of the price in Calcutta. As a consequence of the lowering of freights one-half both these commodities can be sold on the London market about 24 and 20 per centum cheaper than they were in 1872. The freight on linseed amounts now to 14 per centum, on jute to 13 per centum, on cotton to 4.50 per centum, of the Calcutta prices. Hence, the cost of laying down in London of all these various commodities, which constitute the most important part of Indian exports of merchandise, have been very essentially reduced by the decline in ocean freights."

In recent years the reduction of freights has been no longer so considerable. The following statement is taken from the reports of the Imperial Consulate at Madras published recently in Volume II. of the *Deutsches Handelsarchiv* (the ocean freights from Madras to English ports being given for each fifty cubic feet):

Year	Cotton	Indigo
	s. d. s. d.	s. d. s. d.
1888	32 6 to 45 0	60 0 to 75 0
1889	37 6 " 40 0	70 0
1890	37 6 " 45 0	50 0 " 60 0
1891	37 6 " 45 0	67 6
1892	32 6 " 37 6	62 6 " 67 6

The freight, according to the same authorities, on grain amounted for each 20 cwt. to 32s. 6d.; rose in October of the same year to 45s., and fell in the second half of the year 1892 to 22s. 6d. The charges for sugar for the same periods were 35s., 45s., and 23s. 9d. The reduction of freight on the two last articles is much more considerable than that on cotton and indigo. But, in general, the downward tendency of ocean freights appears in recent years, with the exception of the short time of depression in 1889–91, to have been established.

The cost of inland transportation has also seriously declined, to which the completion of the Indian railway system has chiefly contributed. Thus the fertile grain districts of the northern plains of India have, for example, direct railway connection not only with Bombay but with Calcutta. Inasmuch as the owners of these lines are different, it already results from competition that no railway charges very high rates. To this matter the German Consul-General at Bombay drew attention as early as the year 1881.[1] Moreover, one ought not to forget the following facts: India is a possession wholly dependent upon England; there is either state-ownership of railways, or they have a state guarantee of interest. If a deficit exist in the Indian budget through allowances to the railways, it is not covered by England, although the advantages of cheap freights on Indian railways accrue to the English.

[1] *Deutsches Handelsarchiv*, 1881, II. Bd., p. 408.

In addition to the fall in freight rates is the increasing elimination of the middleman. This was a standing complaint of the English merchants heard before the Royal Commission on the Depression of Trade. This phenomenon is especially felt in India; as already mentioned, the Anglo-Indian merchant has become in many cases only a simple agent, or jobber, between the European producer and the Indian dealer, or *vice versa.*

In the face of these facts, how is it with the theory that the fall in the standard of value of a country is favorable to exportation, but unfavorable to importation in the countries, respectively,—a theory which found many defenders[1] before the Royal Gold and Silver Commission, and of which Herr Professor Dr. Friedberg at the sitting of the Prussian House of Deputies on January 25, 1894, said:[2] "This is a simple axiom, that a depreciating standard necessarily encourages the importation of grain (*sc.* into the countries having a gold standard). Gentlemen, the proposition that a cheapened standard serves as a protective tariff for the country concerned, that it acts as an incentive to exports and discourages imports, is so far undeniable that if anyone doubts it, certainly no one can discuss it with him." (Very true! Bravo! from the right). "Indeed, gentlemen, it is one of the most elementary propositions of political economy." This is the somewhat loud repetition of an argument which Nasse disproved in the following words, simpler certainly than his opponents: "The immediate consequence of a change in the relative values of the two metals is a corresponding change in the relative values of (1) the money circulating in countries having a silver standard to (2) that circulating in countries having a gold standard,—which is expressed in the rate of exchange. But if the standard of value of a country depreciates in comparison with that of other lands, only exported and imported articles will first be affected in their relative values by the change. The rising rates of foreign exchange must raise their prices. The relative prices of other commodities, however, are not affected for a con-

[1] Cf. the statements of Barclay, Fielden, Gibbs, McLean, Nicholson, and Tidman.

[2] *Stenographic Report*, p. 122.

siderable time by the change in the value of the home, as compared with the foreign, circulating medium. The wages of labor, and a variety of conditions affecting the prices of articles of daily use are only gradually changed. The further result follows that for a time the production and the exportation of exportable articles obtains an increased profit, and the consumption of imported articles that have become relatively dearer is diminished. The fall in the value of silver, to go on, has made it possible for countries using silver to offer their articles of export on the European market at lower prices than those at which they could formerly furnish them, since their cost of production, reckoned in silver, remained unchanged; on the other hand they received by sale in foreign countries payment in a gold medium, which, in consequence of the change in the relative values of the two metals amounts to a greater quantity of silver money than in the earlier period. The supply of articles for exportation to silver-using countries has, therefore, depressed their price in the world's markets. *Vice versa*, the cessation of exportation to silver-using countries must exercise a certain depressing influence on the price of articles of export in the gold-using countries."

It then became possible, through this shifting of prices, for the Indian producer to extend his exports at the expense of the producer in gold-using countries, but the importation into silver-using countries by the latter (*i. e.*, gold-using countries) was thereby rendered exceedingly difficult, nay often impossible.

In order to establish in how far this theory applies to India we shall have to ascertain how Indian prices have been affected since 1870; what influence the fall of silver has had on the shaping of prices, and how the foreign trade of the country especially has been affected.

As concerns the effect on prices, it would certainly be a great error to suppose that the rates of exchange had remained especially steady in former times, and that prices had undergone great fluctuations only after these changes had come about. The opposite is correct. Owing to the completion of the system of railways, as well as the opening of the Suez Canal, the possibility of quickly replenishing stocks of goods imported from Europe in case of necessity has allowed the working of domestic prices to go on much more regularly. Taking the price in January 1873 as 100, the quotations of gray shirtings fluctuated in India, in 1861–72, between 215 and 93; in 1881–92, only between 84 and 74; of mule twist, No. 40, in 1861–72, between 218 and 77; in 1881–92, between 81 and 62; and of Doodiah wheat, in 1861–72, between 130 and 59; in 1881–92, between 103 and 72. Such differences of prices in the same province, as are found, for instance, in the prices of wheat in Bengal in 1868, are today wholly impossible; at that time one rupee exchanged in Patna for 30.61 seers,[1] while in Hazaribagh, situated in the same province, the famine price of a rupee for 3.77 seers was exacted, or nearly eight times as great as in Patna.

Much more important to us is the question whether the prices of Indian goods reckoned in silver have risen or fallen in the last two decades, or whether they have remained stationary. In the period to 1886, Nasse was able to establish only a slight fall in the prices expressed in silver. In answer to the question how the matter stands today, Mr. J. E. O'Conor, the admirable statistician of the Indian Government, assistant secretary to the Department of Finance and Commerce, laid before the Herschell Committee a short statement which affords satisfactory information.[2] Mr. O'Conor makes use of the method of index numbers and takes the price of March 1873, as 100. The results are shown in Table I, on page 32:

The articles here chosen compose about one-third of the total imports, but a great number of other imported articles follows their price-movements. Because the fluctuations in the price of "gray shirtings" influenced the changes in price not only of unbleached, but also of bleached and colored fabrics. The fluctuations in the price of iron also controlled those of hardwares, machinery, manufacturing implements, and railway supplies.

[1] One seer=2.057 English pounds.

[2] Appendix to *Minutes*, pp. 161 *et seq.*

These selected articles are, therefore, to be regarded as the representatives of at least one-half of the imports, and only this part of the imports really affects the great mass of the population. The other half of the imports consists of goods which are either not articles of necessity, or are mainly consumed by Europeans, or are used in such small quantities that they play no rôle in the domestic economy of the people.

TABLE I. WHOLESALE PRICES OF IMPORTED ARTICLES AT CALCUTTA.

Period	Gray Shirtings 8¼ lbs.	Mule Twist, White, No. 40	Mule Twist, Turkey Red, No. 40	Braziers' Copper	Iron, Flat, Bolt, Bar
1861–1865	145	146	123	99	64
1866–1870	128	122	117	88	69
1871–1875	93	92	104	92	89
1876–1880	79	83	83	88	67
1881–1885	78	77	62	78	61
1886–1890	80	71	57	76	62
1891	74	70	56	72	62
1892	74	64	57	72	64

It can be accepted that the price of woolen goods reckoned in rupees, since 1873, has fallen about 26 per centum, of woolen yarns about 36–43 per centum, of iron about 36 per centum, and of copper about 28 per centum. So far as regards imports.

Mr. O'Conor remarks on these figures: "In general it is to be said that—with the exception of rice, which since 1887 shows a marked tendency to move upward, and of jute—all the important staple articles in the export trade have either not risen or have fallen in price."

This might be a matter for congratulation to us, so far as it concerns articles which we must draw from the tropics and in which we are not competing in India. It is quite a different matter in the case of wheat and spun cotton, but of these later.

It would be a very great error, in my opinion, to assign, as has frequently been done, to the "appreciation of gold"—which is so often asserted, but never proved—the stability or fall of most of the wholesale prices reckoned in silver. First, attention should be called to the following facts: According to the statements of the *Economist* ("Commercial History and Review" for 1873 and 1892) the price of Mule Twist, No. 40, fair, second quality, on March 1, 1873, was 15d.; the price of the same article in January 1892, was 8d. The price therefore has fallen 46.67 per centum. According to our Table I. the cheapening of the price reckoned in silver [in India] of Mule Twist, white, No. 40, between March 1893 and January 1892 was 36 per centum. If we consider the changes meanwhile arising from the relations of gold or silver, it appears that the price of cotton yarn, reckoned in gold in Calcutta has fallen from 1873 to 1892 about 54 per centum. That the downward movement of prices has been more violent in Calcutta than in Manchester becomes clear, in view of the great decline in the cost of transportation which in the last twenty years has affected the exports of English cotton goods to India by a reduction of freight charges and the like.

TABLE II. WHOLESALE PRICES OF ARTICLES OF EXPORT AT CALCUTTA, BOMBAY, AND RANGOON. MARCH 1873=100.

ARTICLES	1861–1865	1886–1870	1871–1875	1876–1880	1881–1885	1886–1890	1891	1892
Cotton, Broach	128	112	87	86	88	90	84	75
Opium { Bengal	104	100	102	98	100	87	81	89
Opium { Malwa	113	114	100	116	101	93	87	88
Rice { Moonghy (Calcutta)	87	111	115	148	104	124	147	162
Rice { Ballam (Calcutta)	88	120	115	154	122	134	143	169
Rice { Ngatsain (Rangoon)	..	...	84	97	126	122	133	156
Rice { Ngakyuok (Rangoon)	..	...	109	113	157	151	164	194
Wheat { Calcutta	82	101	85	94	84	83	87	103
Wheat { Bombay	..	108	79	108	77	94	93	118
Linseed { Calcutta	85	107	104	104	95	104	97	112
Linseed { Bombay	90	104	98	103	97	104	103	110
Jute { Picked	103	110	128	153	132	163	126	236
Jute { Ordinary	88	103	123	144	123	153	115	231
Jute Gunny Bags	97	103	100	94	105	110	93	132
Tea, good Souchong	..	...	110	94	69	54	50	41
Cotton Yarn, 20's	..	...	...	81	77	74	70	65
Cotton Cloth, 44-inch, 24yds., 8 lbs	..	...	...	83	81	77	77	77
Indigo, good	95	102	108	103	110	86	86	74
Hides, "slaughtered"	70	67	96	96	99	81	65	66

The purchasing power, furthermore, of the rupee in recent years appears to have measurably fallen, at least in comparison with those articles which are not objects of foreign trade, especially in comparison with the different kinds of grain. Mr. O'Conor has laid before the Herschell committee the index numbers of retail prices of the most important cereals in the principal markets, taken from the fourteen daily quotations published by the government. Make allowance for the fact that India was afflicted with two serious famines, between 1866 and 1870, and between 1876 and 1880:

TABLE III.

ARTICLES	1861–1865	1866–1870	1871–1875	1876–1880	1881–1885	1886–1890	1891
Rice (10)	103	130	102	140	116	135	149
Wheat (16)	103	133	95	127	96	117	135
Jawar[1] (15)	122	140	100	146	96	122	138
Bajra[1] (15)	120	131	102	147	99	122	137
Ragi[1] (3)	149	185	92	209	103	103	138
Gram (10)	88	149	98	130	93	114	129
Barley (8)	80	108	95	113	90	113	131

The figures in parentheses after the name of each kind of grain is the number of markets from which the quotations of the average prices are reckoned.

As Mr. O'Conor remarks, these index numbers represent the high range of prices for each kind of grain in the districts where they are produced and consumed in the greatest quantities.

The absolute average prices in Seers per rupee are as follows:

TABLE IV.

ARTICLES	1861–1865	1866–1870	1871–1875	1876–1880	1881–1885	1886–1890	1891
Wheat (99)	21.36	15.45	19.46	16.35	19.98	16.05	14.05
Rice (90)	21.66	17.42	19.14	15.30	18 21	15.41	13.91
Jawar (95)	25.78	21.25	25.30	20.42	27.64	21.17	18.44
Barley (54)	35.60	25.81	28.54	26.94	30.48	24.25	20.30
Bajra (86)	24.27	19.90	22.38	18.91	24.22	19.49	16.57
Average of these five kinds of grains.	25.73	19.97	22.96	19.58	24.11	19.28	16.15

[1] Jawar is *Yorghum Vulgare;* Bajra, *Penisetum Typhoideum;* Ragi, *Panicum Milliaceum;* and Gram does not appear as an export.

According to the computations of the *Economist*,[1] on the basis of the Blue-book on *Prices and Wages in India*, the retail prices in rupees per cwt. were as follows:

TABLE V.

Articles	1871–1875	1876–1880	1881–1885	1886–1890	1891
Rice	41.4	47.3	45.8	55.6	62.0
Wheat	42.1	51.7	43.6	52.7	61.3
Barley	28.6	31.8	26.7	33.4	40.0
Jawar	31.2	41.4	29.5	38.4	43.6
Bajra	36.2	46.6	34.5	32.7	48.6
Gram	32.6	38.1	31.2	38.1	44.6

A report to the secretary of state for India, dated October 5, 1892, No. 272, signed by the whole Indian ministry, remarks upon this movement of prices as follows:

"The length and breadth of the country is now traversed by railways, and numerous steamship connections on the coast furnish opportunities for exchange of goods, all of which twenty years ago did not exist. Consequently prices can never sink so low as formerly in times of superabundance, when the demand was merely local and usually less than the supply, and when therefore the price was more or less settled by tradition and custom. Today there are relatively few districts from which grain cannot be easily taken to distant regions, where the supply is less than the demand, or even to foreign lands. The opportunities for trade are today so multiplied that the traders will not dispose of their supplies at low prices in a local market, so long as they know they can obtain higher prices if they export their grain, or send it to another Indian market. Prices are therefore controlled by free competition and by a steadily increasing demand, and in the future they will remain at a higher level.

"The wholesale prices of rice and wheat—the only two cereals—in regard to which exportation, as compared with local demand, plays a considerable part, are to a great extent influ-

[1] September 3, 1892, p. 1120.

enced by the prices of European markets expressed in gold and by the temporary movements of exchange." [Not, however, the reverse!] "As concerns the retail prices of breadstuffs it is to be remarked that in the last three or four years loud complaints have been continually made regarding the high prices of those kinds of grain which serve as the main subsistence of the people."

We can, however, quietly accept the fact that not only have the changed conditions of trade raised the prices of grain, but also that a diminution in the purchasing power of the rupee has contributed to this. This diminution in the purchasing power of the rupee has already extended so far that wages have risen quite considerably in recent years. It is well known that wages especially follow very slowly upon a change in the purchasing power of money; above all, of course, in a country like India which is so much under the control of tradition and custom. Appendix II. in the preliminary report of the Herschell Committee gives the following proof of this:

WAGES IN SKILLED AND UNSKILLED LABOR IN RUPEES, ETC., PER MONTH.

Year	Able-bodied Agricultural Laborer			Percentage if 1873–1876 be 100	Syce or Groom			Percentage	Common Mason, Carpenter, or Blacksmith			Percentage
	R.	A.	P.		R.	A.	P.		R.	A.	P.	
1873–76	6	11	1	100	6	7	3	100	14	9	2	100
1877–81	6	7	11	96	6	7	4	100	14	11	11	101.2
1882–86	6	8	8	97.7	6	11	11	104.5	15	11	10	108
1887–91	7	1	8	106.1	6	15	8	108.1	16	14	5	116

On a stationary purchasing power of silver in India—or of an appreciation of gold, which for many other reasons cannot be accepted—one would hardly lay emphasis in view of the fact that wages, in spite of the increase in population by fully 27.8 millions[1] from 1881 to 1891, have in certain callings risen quite considerably.

[1] *Census Report* of 1891, p. iii. Of course, the figures of population of 1891 on which the above comparison is made, does not include those parts of the country which were incorporated into the Indian Empire only after 1881.

Certainly, what has just been said about the movement of prices does not hold true for that portion of the lowlands where a complete state of barter exists. The report on the census of 1891 remarks on this (p. 97): "It is the absence of all competition which is striking, in regard to all the non-agricultural services rendered to the village community. In the greatest number of cases—and this applies undoubtedly to the whole of India where the village system prevails—services of this kind are paid for either by a transfer of a piece of village land, in which each of these lots is known by the service rendered, or by a fixed amount of grain, etc., from each harvest, for which amount the individual possessors of land must provide. In those cases in which cash is paid, the price is apparently ruled rather by tradition, which yields but slowly to change, than by considerations affecting the value in the open market. There is no incentive for the new people to be progressive, nor to underbid the old. With the improvement of the means of communication and of general security on the roads, perhaps the "higgling of the market"—to use a phrase from political economy—has found its way into the Indian village; but, as a rule, that which is prepared in the village itself and not imported, nor brought for sale to the inter-communal market, is exempt from competition. It is tradition, that, as in the days of Pindar, governs everything.[1]

It is, however, quite another matter, if we turn to the dealer in imported goods and to those who do not belong to the original organism—for they were only connected with the life of the village after that institution ceased to exist—or to the "outsiders," as Sir H. Maine expressed it. They really form a

[1] "Das ganz
Gemeine ist's, das ewig Gestrige,
Was immer war und immer wiederkehrt,
Und morgen gilt, weil's heute hat gegolten,
Denn aus Gemeinem ist der Mensch gemacht
Und die Gewohnheit nennt er seine Amme.
* * * * * * *
Das Jahr übt eine heiligende Kraft,
Was grau vor Alter ist, das ist ihm göttlich."
—Cited from Schiller in the *Report on the Population of East India.*

market, which the same author says was a neutral piece of land, so destined for this purpose that the village communities situated around it and shut in on themselves could meet there. Nowadays, traders of this sort are found in each village, and to the casual observer the impression is given that they stand on the same basis as the rest of the community. But they form no organic part of the real village community, and on the occasion of the village festivals—in which the system appears very exclusive—they have no well-established place. These remarks apply to the shop-keeper, the spice-dealer, the grain-trader, the money-lender (who can be included with those just mentioned), and to the tailor, whose labors are certainly not needed by the greatest part of the population, except in the north where the breech-cloth and the sári have been in great measure supplanted by trousers, for both sexes. All these are in the village, but do not belong to the village. Among these, therefore, methods of barter no longer exist, but an economic monetary system prevails; they form the free market.

B. EXPORTATION OF WHEAT FROM INDIA.

The most serious question for Germany is, How has the exportation of wheat from India been modified since the beginning of the fall of silver? As to that it can be laid down, in spite of all the claims of our landed interests, and in spite of all Professor Friedberg's talk about axioms and the most elementary propositions of political economy, that there cannot be noted the smallest connection between the exportation of wheat from India and the fluctuations in the prices of silver—as appears from Table VII. (p. 39).

It might be of interest here to listen to the views regarding the wheat trade of a most competent judge of the relations involved, the oft-quoted director of the statistical bureau of the Indian Empire, Mr. J. E. O'Conor. In his "Review of the Trade in India in 1891–2" he says:[1]

"Much misapprehension appears still to exist in regard to

[1] *Economist*, "Monthly Trade Supplement," October 15, 1892, p. 10.

the conditions which have permitted the development of the wheat trade and in regard to the progress which it has made. It may be useful, therefore, to recapitulate the facts briefly. They are these: Until the opening of the Suez Canal no trade in wheat was possible, the cost and duration of the transit around the Cape having the double effect of making Indian wheat too dear for the European market and of spoiling it by giving weevils time to do their work of destruction. After the opening of the canal it was

TABLE VII. EXPORTS OF WHEAT FROM INDIA.[1]

Year Ending March 31	Quantity (in 1000 Cwt.)	Value (in 1000 Rx.)	Average Rate of Exchange
			s. d.
1877	5,587	1,958	1 8.51
1878	6,373	2,874	1 8.79
1879	1,057	520	1 7.79
1880	2,202	1,124	1 7.96
1881	7,444	3,278	1 7.96
1882	19,901	8,870	1 7.89
1883	14,194	6,089	1 7.52
1884	21,001	8,896	1 7.54
1885	15,851	6,316	1 7.31
1886	21,069	8,005	1 6.25
1887	22,264	8,626	1 5.44
1888	13,538	5,562	1 4.90
1889	17,610	7,523	1 4.38
1890	13,799	5,791	1 4.57
1891	14,320	6,042	1 6.09
1892	30,303	14,380	1 4.73

discovered that there was still an impediment to the trade in the existence of an export duty of three annas the maund, or, say, about five rupees the ton. On the representation of the Bombay Chamber of Commerce this duty was removed in January, 1873. At that time the quantity exported was only 394,000 cwt., but with the removal of the duty it increased until it exceeded six millions cwt. in 1877. The greatest part of the exports, however, was from Calcutta, for Bombay and Kurrachee were not yet linked by uninterrupted railway communication with the vast wheat fields of the northwestern provinces and the Punjab, whence are now drawn the largest part of the supplies available

[1] Appendix to *Minutes of Indian the Currency Committee*, p. 241. Cf. also the graphic representation at the end of this book.

for export. Then followed the great famine of 1877, 1878, and 1879, raising prices in India to a level that interrupted the export business. With the return of plenty, a reduction of prices, the completion of railway communications, and consequently the reduction of cost of transport, trade was able to take its full development. In 1880–1 the exports were still under 7.50 millions cwt.; in the following year they approached 20 millions. The trade, in fact, owing to the circumstances here mentioned, really began only in 1881–2. Since then there has been no appreciable development. Until 1890–1 the exports were in three of these years only somewhat in excess of those of 1881–2, while in six of these years they were much below them. Last year's exports were abnormal, and it is unlikely that such circumstances will recur soon. Considering the whole trade, it may be said that the average quantity of wheat which Europe will take from us in ordinary times is not quite one million tons, and that we have not on the whole exceeded that quantity since we first supplied it ten years ago."

The exceptionally large exportation of 1891–2 is to be ascribed to the failure in the harvests in Europe, to the Russian interdict on the exportation of grain, and to the resulting rapid rise of price on the European corn markets; as a result, it was exceptionally profitable to export grain from India.

It is to be seen that so weighty an authority as Mr. O'Conor ascribes the exportation of wheat simply to the changed conditions of trade, and does not devote a word to the fall in the price of silver.

Indian wheat, however, is today landed much more cheaply on the European market than twenty years ago, and this also is to be ascribed exclusively to the changed conditions of intercourse and trade. A wholesale merchant, F. Comber, a prominent figure in the Anglo-Indian trade, made definite statements on this point before the Royal Gold and Silver Commission.[1]

The difference of ocean freights is not quite so great here as in the official tables given on page 27, although it is still impor-

[1] *Second Report*, p. 252.

tant enough to explain, in great part, the fall in prices in England. Jubbulpore was already connected by railway with Bombay in 1873; but the cheapening of inland transportation is not therefore alone due to the fact that the corn district in question had only been opened to the markets of the world from about that time; and the fall in freights expressed in English gold is partly to be explained by the fall in the price of silver. No regard has been given to the transportation from the places of production

TABLE VIII. COST OF TRANSPORT OF WHEAT FROM INTERIOR DEPÔTS IN INDIA AND AMERICA TO UNITED KINGDOM, PER QUARTER.

Year	Average Price of Wheat in United Kingdom	Cost of Carriage Indian Wheat: Inland—Jubbulpore to Bombay[1]	Cost of Carriage Indian Wheat: Sea—Bombay to United Kingdom	Cost of Carriage Indian Wheat: Together	Cost of Carriage American Wheat: Inland—Chicago to New York[1]	Cost of Carriage American Wheat: Sea—New York to United Kingdom	Cost of Carriage American Wheat: Together	Reduction Compared with 1873 in: Price of Wheat	Reduction Compared with 1873 in: Transport from India	Reduction Compared with 1873 in: Transport from America
	s. d.	s. d.	s. d.	s. d.	s. d.	s. d.	s. d.	s. d.	s. d.	s. d.
1873	58 8	9 8	13 0	22 8	6 5	7 0	13 5			
1874	55 9	9 7	11 11	21 6	4 8	6 6	11 2	2 11	1 2	2 3
1875	45 2	6 10	11 4	18 2	3 10	6 0	9 10	13 6	4 6	3 7
1876	46 2	6 6	10 6	17 0	3 2	5 6	8 8	12 6	5 8	4 9
1877	56 9	6 7	9 2	15 9	3 9	4 10	8 7	1 11	6 11	4 10
Average of 4 years	51 0	7 4	10 9	18 1	3 10	5 8	9 6	7 8	4 7	3 11
1878	46 5	6 3	4 10	11 1	3 1	5 0	8 1	12 3	11 7	5 4
1879	43 10	6 4	6 3	12 7	3 10	4 2	8 0	14 10	10 1	5 5
1880	44 4	6 4	8 1	14 5	4 1	3 10	7 11	14 4	8 3	5 6
1881	45 4	6 4	9 2	15 6	2 9	2 10	5 7	13 4	7 2	7 10
1882	45 1	6 5	6 10	13 3	2 8	2 7	5 3	13 7	9 3	8 2
Average of 5 years	45 0	6 4	7 0	13 4	3 3	3 8	6 11	13 8	9 3	6 6
1883	41 7	5 8	6 2	11 10	2 10	2 8	5 6	17 1	10 10	7 11
1884	35 8	5 7	4 3	9 10	2 2	2 4	4 6	23 0	12 10	8 11
1885	32 10	5 4	4 10	10 2	1 11	2 2	4 1	25 10	12 6	9 4
1886	31 0	5 1	3 10	8 11	2 11	2 2	5 1	27 8	13 9	8 4
1887 { 1st six mos.	33 11	4 11	4 6	9 5	2 9	1 8	4 5	24 9	13 3	9 0
Average of 4½ years	35 0	5 1	4 9	10 1	2 6	2 2	4 8	23 8	11 7	8 9

[1] This does not include cost of transport from the producing districts to Jubbulpore and Chicago.

to Jubbulpore, which has been very essentially cheapened by the building of roads, railways, and canals.

In addition, there is a very admirable organization of the export trade in grain. The great English firms have their offices at the principal markets in the interior of the great empire, and when the merchant cables from the Metropolitan Corn Exchange in Mark Lane the quotations of wheat to his agent at Jubbulpore or Cawnpore, this agent, on the basis of the railway and ocean freights as well as of the rates of exchange, can immediately compute how much he ought to pay the Zamindar.

By this centralization of the wholesale trade expenses are naturally largely reduced. If attention be further drawn to the fact that transportation from the places of production to the grain markets of the interior has been made very much easier and cheaper by roads, railways, and canals, and that the grain districts of the valleys in northern India are now all connected with the sea, it is nonsense to ascribe the falling or stationary wholesale prices of wheat to the fall in the value of silver either alone or in great part. If we compare the retail prices of wheat given in our Tables III, IV, and V, with those of the wholesale prices contained in Table II, and note how the latter have remained stationary while, on the contrary, the former have risen very considerably, it is impossible to find any other explanation for this than the cheapened cost of movement to the grain markets and the significant reduction of expenses in the wholesale trade.

A genuine creation of myths has appeared in connection with the exports of wheat from India. Dr. Arendt, for example, claims in his *Leitfaden der Währungs-Frage*, p. 31: The English agriculturist was not able to protect himself without customs duties against the agricultural competition of India; and, hence, already more than one-half of the English area is today out of cultivation. This last statement is pre-eminently false. The whole superficies of England amounts to 77,642,099 acres; in which, however, are comprised the numerous waterways particularly in England, as well as extensive districts in Scotland which had been turned into sheep pastures in the last century in consequence of the sad events following the battle of Culloden, and which have later gone entirely out of cultivation. Of the above, there were, in 1892, 47,977,903 acres in cultivation, being 61.8 per centum of the whole area under culture; while in 1871–75 there were only 46,984,106 acres.[1] Since the appearance of Indian competition, therefore, the cultivated area has even increased. On the other hand, it is true that in consequence of international competition the acreage chiefly planted in wheat as well as in other cereals has steadily declined since 1871–75. While, in 1871–75, 3,737,140 acres were planted in wheat, and 11,543,577 acres in other cereals; in 1892 the figures were, respectively, 2,298,607 and 9,328,701 acres. Furthermore, the income from land deduced from the schedules of the income tax has fallen from 1877 to 1892 from £69,438,632 to £57,391,846, undoubtedly in consequence of international competition. There were, from 1877 to 1892, 1225.19 millions cwt. of wheat and wheat-flour imported into the United Kingdom, of which 120.79 millions cwt., or 9.86 per centum, were imported from India.[2]

It would now be exceedingly interesting to learn from Dr. Arendt on what ground he concludes that it is precisely the 9.86 per centum, and not the other 90.14 per centum, of wheat imports —since as regards wheat we are here concerned solely with Indian competition—which has injured the English producers of grain. Or is he, perhaps, putting forth a theory of "marginal losses" on the analogy of marginal utilities ?

But another main argument, also, of our bimetallistic agrarians is good for nothing—the argument that it is impossible for our agricultural interests to compete with the grain from silver-using countries, because it receives a premium on export due to the fall in the value of silver. India being the only silver country from

[1] All these figures are taken from the *Agricultural Returns for Great Britain*, 1892.

[2] These figures are taken from the *Statistical Abstracts for the United Kingdom* 1877-91 and 1878-92.

which Europe draws grain—in foreign trade America and Roumania pay gold, Russia, Austria-Hungary, and the La Plata states as yet have solely a paper, not a silver standard—it is exactly in India where we see that (1) the fall in the price of silver has not had the slightest influence upon the exports of wheat; that (2) rather the purchasing power of the rupee in recent years as compared with grain has declined quite considerably (and in reality fell similarly with the quotations of silver); that (3) the cheapening of Indian grain on the European market is to be ascribed to the improvement and the cheapening of means of communication, as well as of a better organization of trade; and finally that (4) India does not control the price of grain on the European market,—but, quite the reverse, grain is only exported from India when the character of the Indian harvests and the European quotations of prices make it profitable.

C. THE COTTON INDUSTRY.

To England by far the most important part of the trade with India is in cotton goods. To be sure, it is no longer as it was up to the seventies when more than one-half of the whole Indian imports consisted of English cotton goods; but even yet fully 41 per centum of the total imports into India in 1891-2 were products of the Lancashire industries. About 300 millions rupees of English cotton goods have been on the average imported into India each year since 1886. Mr. O'Conor calls the

EXPORTS OF COTTON YARN AND COTTON CLOTHS TO INDIA AND EASTERN ASIA.

Year	Yarn in Millions of English Lbs.				
	Total Exports	To India		To China, Japan, Straits, etc.	
	Lbs.	Lbs.	Per Cent.	Lbs.	Per Cent.
1887	251.0	51.5	20.52	35.3	14.06
1889	252.3	48.6	19.26	35.7	14.15
1890	258.4	52.5	20.32	38.1	14.75
1891	245.5	53.2	21.67	28.0	11.40
1892	233.2	42.1	18.05	31.9	13.68

Year	Cloth in Millions of Yards				
	Total Exports	To India		To China, Japan, Straits, etc.	
	Yds.	Yds.	Per Cent.	Yds.	Per Cent.
1887	4904.0	1973.4	40.24	763.0	15.56
1889	5001.5	2138.7	42.76	759.2	15.18
1890	5124.2	2189.6	42.73	806.7	15.74
1891	4912.6	1964.8	40.00	823.2	16.76
1892	4873.3	1974.6	40.52	779.6	15.99

importation of cotton goods the backbone of the Indian imports; and, similarly, it can be said that this importation, together with that to the rest of eastern Asia, is the backbone of the exports from Lancashire. This is shown by the above tables.

For some years the English cotton manufacturers have complained of the excessive losses caused by the fall of the price of silver to their exports to Eastern Asia. Without doubt the prices of their manufactures have heavily fallen, as the following extract from the *Economist* tables of prices shows:

Year	Mule No. 40 Fair 2d Quality	Gold End Shirtings 40 in. 66 Reeds 37½ yds. 8 lbs. 12 oz.
	d.	s. d.
1873, January 1	15	11 3
1877, " 1	11½	9 10½
1883, " 1	9¾	7 10½
1887, " 1	8⅜	7 4
1892, September 1	7	7 0[1]
1893, January 1	8¼	7 10½

Yet, according to the statements of the *Economist*, the profits of the spinning mills were not bad. It gives the following figures for the largest stock companies (see next page):

The bad results of the two last years are explained, according to the statements of the *Economist*, by the fact that in 1891, in expectation of a small crop of cotton in America, the manufacturers laid in their raw material at high prices; but when the crops turned out unexpectedly good, the price of cotton as a consequence fell excessively, and the manufacturers found they

[1] Lowest point.

Year	Number of Factories		For Each Factory
		£	£
1892	90	Loss 101,434	1127
1891	93	Gain 10,763	115
1890	90	" 376,041	4178
1889	86	" 220,587	2565
1888	85	" 250,932	2952
1887	88	" 85,810	975
1886	90	Loss 61,718	615
1885	87	" 2,730	31
1884	60	Gain 125,000	2083

had made a serious mistake. In 1892 took place the greatest stoppage of labor which had ever been seen in Lancashire—first, the Stalybridge lock-out, which brought to a standstill for three weeks 18 million spindles, and then the great strike which lasted from November 7, 1892, to March 1893, during which time 15 million spindles were idle. In 1892 something more than ¾ of one per cent. was earned on the large working capital of the factories just mentioned (£3,629,078 of capital stock, including on the average £3,441,028 loans bearing 4½ per cent. interest). In 1891 there was paid an average dividend on the capital stock of 6s. per £100; in 1890, of £10 18s.; in 1889, of £6 12s. 6d.; and in 1888, £7 8s. 3d. It is to be seen from this that the Lancashire industries can subsist in spite of the lowered value of silver, and notwithstanding the fact that one-half their exports go to silver-using countries; although I will not wholly deny that a higher rate for silver would be very much more favorable for them, and that, as formerly mentioned, they suffer severely from violent fluctuations of the exchanges. This industry with its exceptionally large capital has been, to the present time, precisely in the condition to make up every fall of price, to a certain extent, by improvements in processes, and by larger investments of capital.

And, in the main, it was not the fall in the price of silver which drove the English cotton manufacturers into the bimetallic camp; it was, for the most part, rather the fear of the extremely flourishing industry in India which was competing against them, and whose immense progress was ascribed to the fall in silver acting as a protective tariff. And, in reality, there is every reason for Lancashire to look with anxiety on the spinning and cotton-cloth mills at Bombay, whose growth is truly astonishing.

INDIAN COTTON INDUSTRY.

YEAR	Factories	Spindles	Looms	EXPORTS	
				Yarn (in 1000 lbs.)	Cloth (in 1000 yds.)
1876–77	47	1,100,112	9,139	7,927	15,544
1880–81	58	1,471,730	13,283	26,901	30,424
1884–85	81	2,037,055	16,455	65,897	47,909
1887–88	97	2,375,739	18,840	113,451	69,486
1888–89	108	2,670,022	22,156	128,907	70,265
1889–90	114	2,934,637	22,078	141,950	59,496
1890–91	125	3,197,740	23,845	169,275	67,666
1891–92	127	3,272,988	24,670	161,253	73,384

EXPORT OF COTTON YARN AND COTTON GOODS FROM THE UNITED KINGDOM TO CHINA, HONG KONG AND JAPAN.[1]

Year	Yarn in 1000 lbs.	Cloth in 1000 yds.
1877	33,086	394,484
1880	46,426	509,099
1884	38,856	439,937
1887	35,354	618,146
1888	44,643	652,404
1889	35,720	557,004
1890	37,869	633,606
1891	27,971	595,258

Indian spinning mills have, in particular, grown rapidly in the last 15 years, and they have entirely beaten the English on the Eastern Asiatic market; on the other hand, England still entirely controls Eastern Asia in cotton cloth. These facts affords us efficient guidance as to where we have to search for the reasons why the Indian cotton industry has shot up so extraordinarily.

The manufacturers of Lancashire claim, as already mentioned that the fall of silver is solely responsible for it. Mr. J. C

[1] These tables, taken from the Appendix to the *Minutes of Indian Currency Committee*, p. 244, do not wholly agree with those of the *Economist*, because the latter includes Java, Straits Settlements, etc.

Fielden, a prominent leader of the Manchester bimetallists, tried to explain the phenomenon before the Royal Gold and Silver Commission,[1] as follows: At the end of 1885 good Dhollera cotton cost on the Bombay market 180 rupees per candy of 784 pounds. At the same time yarn 20's cost at Bombay 6⅜ annas per pound. If it is reckoned that 116 pounds of raw cotton is used to make 100 pounds of yarn, the following results are reached:

(1) Exchange, 2s. Per Rupee.

	Rs.		s.	d.
For 100 lbs. yarn is received - - - -	39.84	=	79	8¼
116 lbs. raw cotton costs - - - -	26.63	=	53	3¼
Leaving for the spinner - - - -	13.21	=	26	5
	= 3.17d. per lb.			

(2) Exchange, 1s. 6d. per rupee.

	Rs.		s.	d.
For 100 lbs. yarn is received - - - -	39.84	=	59	9¼
116 lbs. raw cotton costs - - - -	26.63	=	39	11½
Leaving for the spinner - - - -	13.21	=	19	9¾
	= 2.47d. per lb.			

Mr. Fielden now says, furthermore, that the Lancashire spinner cannot produce under 2–2¼d. per pound. But the freight is ¾d.; consequently, at a rate of 2s. to the rupee he makes a fair profit, while at a rate of 1s. 6d. he is no longer able to compete with the Indian.

At first sight this argument has about it something very taking, but on going to the bottom of the matter one finds much to suspect. Apart from the fact that the rupee has never, in the last 30 years, reached a rate of 2s.—this rate especially at the present time being unattainable—it seems as if the freight was set somewhat low at ¾d. When cotton in Bombay costs 180 rupees per candy, in Manchester it costs considerably more. The Lancashire spinner has still to pay for the pressing of the cotton in India, ocean freight to Liverpool, insurance, commission to the broker on the cotton exchange, insurance against rates of exchange, and railway transportation from Liverpool to Man-

[1] *Second Report*, p. 129.

chester. Then he has to pack the cotton yarn when ready, and provide for freight, insurance, etc. And can all this be done for ¾d. per pound? Mr. Comber, himself the head of a house engaged in the trade between Lancashire and India—whose interesting testimony before the Gold and Silver Commission will be presently discussed—gives the expenses of transportation as 1.19d. If we take the average between the statements of Messrs. Comber and Fielden, and reckon the cost of freight at about 1d., then the Lancashire spinner, at a rate of 2s. to the rupee, would just about cover his cost; at a rate of 1s. 10⅝d. (the quotation corresponding to the ratio of 1 : 15½) he would have a small loss. But there is yet an additional consideration. Mr. Fielden, in his computation, starts from prices as they were at a time when the rate was 1s. 6d.; but at a rate of 2s. the Indian spinner could also work more cheaply; his manufacturing plant would stand him considerably less; for interest and sinking-fund on the capital contributed in gold he would have to produce much less; he would obtain his coal, which he has to bring from England, cheaper; he would undoubtedly hire his European employees at lower salaries; and, in short, he could save largely in expenses. It cannot possibly be proved by Mr. Fielden's figures that it was the fall in the price of silver which made competition with Bombay impossible for the English cotton spinners.

As opposed to this idea let us note the statement of Mr. Comber, the one frequently referred to previously, before the Gold and Silver Commission.[1] He says (Question 8220): "I quite disagree with the opinion that the large development of the cotton industry in India is due entirely, or even chiefly to the fall in silver. I desire to say that, on the contrary, the Indian mills derive only a trifling and temporary benefit from the changed relations between gold and silver, and that their remarkable development of late years is due chiefly to other and natural advantages which the Indian spinner enjoys over his Lancashire competitor in the production, not of all kinds of yarn, but of those descriptions which can be made from Surat cotton, that is

[1] *Second Report*, pp. 141 *et seq.*

Indian cotton. Before entering into details, I may state broadly that these advantages arise principally from the Indian spinners' proximity to the place where (1) the cotton he uses is grown, and (2) the yarn he spins is consumed."

Mr. Comber then proceeds to explain that a readjustment similar to that which is going on between Lancashire and India is showing itself in the United States. Here the cotton industry is moving more and more from the North to the cotton-producing states of the South, in spite of the fact that both the North and South possess the same currency and even the same high protective tariff system.[1] He gives the following tables:

	Southern States of Union		India	
	Spindles	Looms	Spindles	Looms
1886–7	1,213,346	27,963	2,421,290	18,536
1879–80	579,320	12,329	1,461,590	13,502
Increase	654,026	15,634	959,700	5,034
Increase per cent.	117	127	65⅔	37⅓

CONSUMPTION OF RAW COTTON.

COTTON DELIVERED TO MILLS, IN THOUSANDS OF BALES.

	1886–7	1880–81	Increase	Increase per centum
Northern States	1727	1710	17	1
Southern States	398	205	193	94
India	726	379	347	91

And, as in India, it is distinctly the coarser grades which are produced in the southern states of the North American republic.

Another statement laid before the Commission by the same authority is very interesting, because it clearly shows that it is

[1] "As the Northern mills enjoy equally with the Southern the advantage of protective duties, and have increased during the six years to so small an extent, it is clear that the development of the Southern mills is not due to protection, but to the advantage which they possess in common with the Indian mills, viz., proximity to the areas of production of raw and consumption of manufactured cotton."—Comber, *ibid.*, p. 141.

chiefly the difference in cost of transportation which has favored the Indian cotton industry as against the English. Although Mr. Comber is in the very center of the trade between Lancashire and India, and is thereby so much the more trustworthy, yet in spite of this he does not believe—as do most of those having interests in Manchester, who hope by changes in currency legislation to bring ruin upon their Indian competitors—that he should ascribe the cause of the prosperity of this annoying spinning industry of India to the fall in silver, without a further examination, or at least not on so slight a one as Mr. Fielden's.

COMPARISON BETWEEN COST TO ENGLISH AND TO BOMBAY SPINNERS OF PRODUCING AND LAYING DOWN IN THE EAST, 1 LB. OF 20'S YARN.—EXCHANGE 1S. 5D.

	Cost to		Advantage to	
	English Spinner	Indian Spinner	English Spinner	Indian Spinner
	d.	d.	d.	d.
Cotton, 1¼ lb.	5.69	5	......	0.69
Depreciation and interest on mill and machinery	0.42	0.64	0.22	......
Coals	0.05	0.16	0.11	......
Wages	1.11	0.99	......	0.12
Stores	0.28	0.46	0.18	......
Sundries	0.40	0.25	......	0.15
Cost at mill	7.95	7.50	0.51	0.96
Packing and carriage to Bombay	0.50	......	......	0.50
Delivered at Bombay	8.45	7.50	0.51	1.46
Net advantage	......	......	......	0.95
Packing and carriage to China	0.70	0.26	......	0.44
Delivered in China	8.65	7.76	0.51	1.40
Net advantage	......	......	......	0.89

It will therefore be taken for granted that the Indian spinner has an especial advantage through a saving in the cost of transportation. That labor is cheaper in India is not admitted by all the experts. Wages, it is true, are much lower and the hours of labor are considerably longer; but here again it appears quite distinctly "that cheap labor does not in the least mean cheap production; that on the contrary a low cost of production and a high rate of wages go hand in hand."[1] It is generally conceded that from three and a half to five times as many operatives are needed in India as in Lancashire to care for the same number of spindles. Add to this the high cost of superintendence; a superintendent is necessarily a European at an enormous salary—an expense which plays no part at Manchester, or Oldham. Yet it is credibly asserted that the Indian laborers have improved in recent years; wages in Bombay have correspondingly increased very largely. The cost of a mill-plant in India is naturally much higher than in England, because everything must be obtained from Europe. Mr. Fielden estimated in 1887 the average cost per spindle in Bombay at about £3, and in England 22s. to 25s. Coal must also be brought from England, and is three or four times dearer in India than in Lancashire.

That it is essentially cheaper cost of transportation which has raised the Indian industry to such a height also appears from the following: There is unanimity in the opinion that Lancashire is not capable of competing except in the coarser kinds of yarn up to about 28's or 32's, while now as well as formerly it controls not only the Indian but the east Asian markets in the fine numbers, and its exports of cloths hither might have even risen very considerably. As regards the former, it is precisely the raw material and the cost of transportation which play the principal rôle; while in the finer grades, for which the skilled labor and climate of Lancashire are necessary, India cannot compete.

The English, however, purposely pass over in silence an important consideration by which the depreciation of silver has certainly been of advantage to the British cotton industry. In the Indian cotton mills the capital invested is mainly English, with a little Indian; and there is no doubt that English capitalists would have invested their money in so profitable an industry to a far greater extent, if they had not had—as is commonly complained of in India—a very justifiable dread of investments in countries in which their interest is paid in silver and where they never know how many pounds sterling they shall receive,

[1] J. Schoenhof, *The Economy of High Wages*, New York, 1892, p. 31.

but are almost certain to obtain each year less gold for their income in rupees. *If India had had no depreciating standard, their industries would surely have had a very much larger capital at their disposal, and the competition would have been much sharper and one more keenly felt by Lancashire.*

It should, furthermore, not escape attention that the extent of the market for machine-made cotton goods in India is comparatively limited. Only in the cities are they generally consumed, and the urban population amounted, at the last census, only to something over 27 millions out of 287 millions; thus pretty nearly the whole agricultural population satisfy their demands from the products of domestic industry, which in India is very ancient. Hunter[1] remarks on this:

"While the cotton industry in England dates back only a few centuries we find it in India by the time of the Mahábhárata. The Greek word for cotton, σίνδον, is etymologically the same as the name for India, or Sind; while in later days Calicut on the Malabar coast has given its name to calico. Cotton cloth was always the only material for Indian clothing, with the exception of Assam and Burma, where silk is preferred; perhaps this is a relic of a lost trade with China. The writer of Περίπλους, our oldest authority on Indian trade, names a great number of cotton fabrics under the exports; and Marco Polo, the first Christian traveler, dwells upon the cotton and linen of Cambay. When European adventurers found their way to India, cotton and silk always formed the main contents of the rich cargoes which they brought home. The English especially appear to have been very careful to establish their earliest settlements in close proximity to a weaving population, as at Surat, Calicut, Masulipatam, Hugli. In delicacy of texture, in purity and artistic quality of color, in gracefulness of design the Indian fabrics have yet to find their equal in the whole world. Yet as regards cheapness, they could not hold out against the competition of Manchester. A variety of circumstances worked together to injure the local industry. In the last century England shut the

[1] Hunter, *The Indian Empire*, p. 470.

Indian cotton fabrics out of its markets, not by duties, but by a series of statutes which forbade the wearing of imported cotton goods.[1]

"A change in fashion in the West Indies, after the abolition of slavery, took away the best remaining customer, and meanwhile the products of Lancashire cheapened by improvements in machinery were coming to the front. In more recent times, although the high price of raw cotton during the War of Secession was of profit to the cotton-growers, it almost entirely ruined the local trade in fabrics in the districts producing cotton. In addition to this the necessity, under which England lay, to export to India something to pay for the various imports, gave to this branch of trade constantly an artificial and inflated character.

"From these considerations we find that hand-weaving even yet maintains its position, although certainly with varying success in different parts of the empire. The trade in it has become unprofitable. Little is manufactured for export and the makers of the finer sorts are disappearing. The far-famed muslins of Dacca and Arvi are now nearly extinct specialties; but although as a rural industry weaving is carried on everywhere, it cannot be said that it is flourishing. Even if the Manchester goods are cheaper, yet the domestic fabrics are generally regarded as more durable. Comparative statistics are naturally unattainable, but according to approximate estimates three-fifths of the cotton cloths worn in the country are woven either from domestic or imported yarn."

So says Mr. Hunter, one of the best authorities on the country. If the domestic industry continues even yet in Germany, how can it vanish in an instant in a country so exceptionally conservative as India?

It is also interesting to note what is told by the census of 1891 concerning hand-weaving. According to the enumeration of 1891 not less than 8,820,466 persons lived by the manufacture of cotton fabrics,[2] of whom about 120,000 laborers

[1] Hunter, *ibid.*, p. 448.

[2] If we reckon five to a family, this gives over 1,760,000 cotton operatives.

(including their families, about 600,000 persons) were engaged in the modern establishments equipped with machinery. The *Census Report*[1] thereupon remarks, according to the statements of Mr. Stuart, Census Commissioner of Madras, that the house-industry has slowly grown in the last ten years; and that from the material collected regarding castes it is deduced that this increase is recruited from the classes which do not belong to the castes in which the cotton industry is traditional. He concludes from this that, although the increase is but slight, there is something to be earned in this occupation. The domestic product, although strong and coarse, is clean and durable, and still controls the rural markets, especially among the small farmers,—a fact which strikes everyone who may go but once into the country districts. But in the cities the foreign competition is undoubtedly keener, for the finer products of the hand-loom must be much dearer than those made by European machinery, because the task of the laborer is now so simplified, and the freights are so low; and it is the dweller in cities who is first accessible to innovations. Therefore, if we consider what a small fraction of the population lives in cities and how few of the country people wear fine garments, it does not appear as if the common hand-weaver could be driven out of the field by any competition whatever. Only the maker of muslins and of those airy stuffs which the Anglo-Indians call "woven-air," have to suffer.

D. THE MOVEMENT OF TRADE IN GENERAL.

It would carry us too far afield to treat here singly the other chief articles of Indian foreign trade; it will be sufficient to briefly run over the products whose exports or imports amount to more than a million Rx. In the order of their importance[2] these are as follows:

EXPORTS.

Raw cotton	16.5	Grains	9.3
Rice	12.9	Opium	9.3

[1] P. 105.

[2] The figures are in millions of Rx. for the year 1890–1.

EXPORTS.—*Continued.*

Raw jute	7.6	Indigo	3.0
Cotton twist and yarn	6.6	Cotton cloth	2.9
Wheat	6.0	Jute fabrics	2.5
Tea	5.5	Raw wool	1.6
Hides and pelts	4.7	Coffee	1.5

IMPORTS.

Cotton cloth	27.2	Woolen goods	1.8
Cotton yarn	3.8	Coals	1.5
Sugar	3.4	Provisions	1.5
Oils	2.6	Silk goods	1.4
Iron	2.6	Wearing apparel	1.3
Machinery	2.1	Iron and steel goods	1.2
Railway supplies	2.0	Raw silk	1.1
Copper	1.8		

If we now examine the movement of trade in general since 1881–2—after the consequences of the great famine had disappeared—we find that the total exports of merchandise from India rose [in the ten years ending 1890–1] from 81.9 millions Rx. to 108 millions Rx., or 32 per centum; while, on the other hand the imports of merchandise in the same decade rose from 47.0 millions Rx. to 66.6 millions Rx., or 41.7 per centum. The very fact that the imports into India rose nearly 10 per centum more than the exports might in a measure serve to destroy belief in the thesis—so irrefutably established according to the views of German agrarians and of Professor Friedberg—that a depreciating standard favors exports and discourages imports. If this theory were true, it ought above all to appear in the trade of India with those countries that meet their obligations to foreign nations in gold. Among the gold-standard countries with which India trades the United Kingdom naturally stands foremost. How has the trade with her developed since 1881–2? In 1881–2, the exports of merchandise from India to Great Britain and Ireland amounted to 34.9 millions Rx., in 1891–2, to 34.6 millions Rx., or even a slight decline. The imports, on the other hand, from the mother-country to the colony rose from 38.7 millions Rx. to 48.3 millions Rx., or nearly

25 per centum. Likewise the exports from India to France remained constant from 1881 to 1890 at about 8 millions Rx.; until the year 1891–2, with its exceptionally large exports of wheat, caused a rise to 11 millions Rx. The exports to Germany, on the contrary, rose sharply from 758,393 Rx. to 5,091,165 Rx.; and imports from 78,252 Rx. to 1,524,969 Rx. All in all, in spite of Professor Friedberg's axiom and most elementary proposition of political economy, the above mentioned theory has not in the least proved true of India, which has had a decidedly depreciated standard of value; and we must accept Nasse's words: "It is not probable that Indian articles of export would have been brought in very much less quantity to the European markets and there sold at higher prices, if India had had the same standard as the nations of Western and Central Europe, or if the ratio of silver to gold had not changed since 1873."

CHAPTER III.

THE FINANCIAL CONDITION OF THE EAST INDIAN GOVERNMENT.—COMPLAINTS OF ITS OFFICIALS.

§ I. THE CONDITION OF THE GOVERNMENT.

At an early period the Indian Government clearly recognized what a serious danger threatened it through the depreciation of silver. In the beginning of 1876, Sir William Muir had already said in his report upon the budget for 1876–7: "The sudden depreciation in the value of silver and the consequent embarrassment of the Indian Government, which is annually obliged to pay in England a sum of about 15 millions pounds sterling in gold, is undoubtedly fraught with great danger in the future. In truth, it can be said that this danger, from whatever point of view we may regard it, is the greatest which has ever threatened Indian finances. War, famine, drought have often visited far greater losses upon the treasury than the damage incurred this year by the fall in the price of silver. But such calamities pass by; the loss is distinctly ascertained and limited; if it is covered, then the finances again stand upon a sure and stable basis. This, however, is not the case here; the immediate effect of the fall of silver is already serious enough, as has been shown. But that which makes the matter so exceptionally important is that no one can foresee the end. The future is wrapped in uncertainty."

This hits the nail on the head. It is not so much the extent of the loss as it is the uncertainty, and the impossibility of making estimates approximating in a slight degree to the truth, which presents such exceptional difficulties to the Indian minister of finance. The ordinary revenue of India all comes in in silver, except about £200,000, which is paid in England in gold at the India office in a number of small items On the other hand,

India has to pay annually about 15 or 16 millions pounds sterling in England. Now if the rate for rupees falls, naturally more silver rupees must be sent in order to make up an equal sum of gold. In 1873–4, before the depreciation of silver began, there was to be paid[1] in gold £13,285,678; at a rate of 1s. 10.351d. to a rupee it amounted to Rx. 14,265,700. In 1892–3, the gold obligations stood at £16,532,215; the estimates supposed a rate of 1s. 4d. and counted upon a surplus of Rx. 146,600; yet the rate fell to 1s. 2,985d., and although the income rose above the estimates by about Rx. 1,653,300, a deficit resulted of Rx. 1,081,-900. These items of expenditure which, in 1873–4, had required, Rx. 17,751,920, took, in 1892–3, Rx. 26,478,415. The estimates for 1893–4 (published before the closing of the mints), taking the rate of exchange at 1s. 2¾d., show a deficit of Rx. 1,595,100.

Thus Sir D. Barbour[2] rightly says: "Our financial situation is dependent on the mercy of the exchanges, and of those in whose power it lies to influence the price of silver. If we assume for the present budget a deficit of Rx. 1,595,100, and then the rate of exchange rises one penny, we shall have a surplus; if it falls to the same extent, the deficit will amount to more than Rx. 3,000,000. If we increase the taxes by Rx. 1,500,000 then a revolution of the wheel can oblige us to again increase the taxes by no less a sum; then comes a change again, and we find that no increase of taxes at all was necessary. Hence it is clear from what has been said that it is a question, to be considered when adopting our measures for next year, not so much of an increase of the revenues or of a reduction of a part of the public expenditures which lie under our control, as it is a question of the chances for an effective regulation of the currency question."

This is quite true; but, notwithstanding, the Indian Government must study how to strengthen its financial position irrespective of the currency question. Before we examine the

[1] *Report of the Indian Currency Committee*, §§ 3 *et seq.*

[2] *Financial Statement* for 1893–4, p. 15, § 31.

items of the budget one by one, permit me to briefly explain in what manner the gold payments are made in England.

A. MEANS OF OBTAINING GOLD.

Payments in gold[1] are made by the "India Council" in London selling through the Bank of England to bankers and merchants, who have to remit to India, council-bills payable, in rupees or telegraphic transfers, on the Treasury at Calcutta, Bombay, and Madras, which ever is desired.

It was not always so. When the Crown took away the Government of India from the East India Company, and found itself obliged to make large gold payments in England, it originally preferred to make gold loans, because the remittance of coin was impracticable. Between 1857 and 1862 the Indian debt in sterling thus rose from £4,000,000 to £35,000,000. At that time, the foreign trade of the country did not make the show it does today; the exports of merchandise were not very much larger than the imports, and remittances of the precious metals could convert a favorable into an unfavorable balance. If we include shipments of the precious metals between May 1, 1855 and April 30, 1862, the imports exceeded the exports. Then, in consequence of the American War, came the immense prosperity of India; in the years 1862 to 1865, the annual excess of exports (including the precious metals) amounted to Rx. 13,500,000. Since then, until 1893, in spite of the great movement of silver from Europe, the Indian exports continually exceeded the imports—as is quite explicable in a country regularly obliged to send abroad interest on its debt; the traders therefore, had to remit to India, annually large sums as an equivalent for the surplus value of exports over imports—sums, which in reality equaled the amount which the Government had to pay in England. Since then, the Indian Government has found it possible to offset their demands for gold remittances over against those of trade and thus by simple exchange operations avoid the sending of coin. This, therefore, presents a method by means of

[1] Palgrave, *Dictionary of Political Economy*, article "Councils Bills."

which the merchants engaged in trade between England and India—or, more correctly, their bankers—procure the ready money which the Indian Government needs to meet their obligations, while the latter covers the payments of merchants in India.

Formerly, these council-bills consisted exclusively of bills of exchange, which the Bank of England put on sale each Wednesday, in regard to which, however, it was usually provided that only a fixed amount on Madras would be furnished. But this became gradually modified because the establishment of a telegraphic connection with India completely changed the character of the trade. The bill of exchange involved too much time, and the Indian Government found that it received more for telegraphic transfers than for exchange; for this reason it decided, in January 1882, to sell telegraphic transfers as well as bills. From the beginning these telegraphic transfers were in good demand, and now their amount generally exceeds the bills, especially when there is a pressing demand for money on the Indian money market. There is a further innovation in that remittances can also be had on another day than Wednesday; it became the practice to allow further sales on Thursday, which allowed the banks to complete their remittances by paying a slight increase in comparison with the Wednesday sales. The Bank of England makes known from time to time in the reports of the money markets in the newspapers what the lowest price is, what amounts are for sale, and how much is sold.

The sales of the India Office should not be regarded from any other point of view than that there remains to the Indian Government,—which has to pay quite a large part of its current expenditures in England, and that too in gold—only the choice (if it is unwilling to create debt continually) of either remitting silver to India, or of selling bills or telegraphic transfers. Now since India has had to the present time a favorable balance of trade, and since the receivers of Indian goods must therefore buy more bills on India than are created by the merchandise dealings, it would have been in the highest degree foolish for the

Indian Government to have followed the former method—*i. e.*, remit silver. That the council-bills depress the price of silver is, of course, true, since they diminish the demand for silver; but if we comprehend that the Indian Government would remit silver and sell it in London in order to meet its obligations in gold, the effect on the silver market in that case would not be any more favorable.

The sale of government bills conforms simply to the needs of the Indian Government for gold. Mr. Arendt[1] is in error in saying: when the sale of Indian Government exchange increases, the price of silver falls, and *vice versa;* "he who has eyes" ought to be able to see this from the figures given in his own statements. It is true, of course, that the amount of exchange payable in silver must increase with every fall in the price of silver, in order that the same amount of gold can be bought as formerly. But Mr. Arendt does not limit himself to this. In general, he does not give the figures of the council-bills in silver but uses as the basis of his argument figures in pounds sterling. Here I may be permitted to ask, from where has Mr. Arendt taken the figures with which he intends to prove his proposition. All his other figures, so far as I can audit them, including those on the sales of council-bills from 1870–75, are correct. But the figures for the sale of council-bills in the years 1876–81 are wrongly stated. Mr. Arendt gives for the six years 11.51, 8.64, 13.98, 14.70, 15.48, and 16.27 millions pound sterling; while the correct figures for 1875–6 to 1880–1 are 12.39, 12.70, 10.13, 13.95, 15.26, and 15.24 millions pounds sterling.[2] If Mr. Arendt had used the correct figures here, he could not have reached his false conclusion as to the connection of the depreciation of silver with the increase of council bills.

We intend to further treat these expenditures of India in England in more detail.

[1] Otto Arendt *Open Letter to Ludwig Bamberger*, Berlin, 1882, p. 50.

[2] See the tables at the end of the book which have been taken from the official, English sources. Arendt quoted formerly the figures of the fiscal years 1869–70 to 1874–5.

B. THE EXPENDITURES OF THE GOVERNMENT.

(a) TO BE PAID IN GOLD (HOME CHARGES).

Let me previse that these expenditures to be paid in gold are designated in the Indian budget in the following manner: First is given the amount in pounds sterling, then comes a heading "exchange," and the sum of both of them gives the amount in English pounds of reckoning (Rx.). This is derived from the fact that the Indian statistics originally regarded the pound sterling as equal to ten rupees, a supposition which has no real justification, because the parity of the rupee at a price for silver of 60⅞d. per ounce is 1s. 10⅝d. In 1891–2 the rate which the Secretary for India obtained at his sales of council-bills and telegraphic transfers was 1s. 4.793d.; and under "exchange" is given in the budget Rx. 6,973,213. In 1892–3 there was a revised estimate of 1s. 3d. ("exchange," Rx. 9.938,200); in the budget for 1893–4, 1s. 2¾d. ("exchange," Rx. 9,935,900).

The total expenditures of the Indian Government in England amounted, in 1891–2, to £15,974,699; in 1892–3, to £16,563,-600; and for 1893–4 they are estimated at £15,843,800. About 15–16 millions pounds sterling have the expenditures of the Indian Government in England oscillated for a series of years; they form, therefore, a very important part of the current expenses, which annually must be paid in the mother country.

The most dangerous thing about it is that the largest items —the payments for interest on the national and railway debts contracted in gold—show a tendency to rise, because the Indian Government is obliged for the most part to place its loans in England. The increase of the burden would have been more seriously felt, if it had not been possible for India to make a very considerable saving in recent years by conversions. Since 1887 there remain only 3 and 3½ per centum Indian sterling loans, which bear about the same rate as the German national debt, which pays ½ per centum more. India, therefore, has unusually high credit on its gold loans; but on its silver loans it has to pay nearly ¾ per centum of interest more, as the annexed table[1] shows:

[1] Appendix to *Indian Currency Committee*, p. 272.

QUOTATIONS OF INDIAN NATIONAL DEBT.

YEAR	4 PER CENT. RUPEE LOAN				Quotations of India Council-Bills		INDIAN STERLING LOAN					
	Quotations in Calcutta		Quotations in London				4 Per Cent.		3½ Per Cent.		3 Per Cent.	
	Highest	Lowest	Highest	Lowest			Highest	Lowest	Highest	Lowest	Highest	Lowest
					d.	d.						
1873	105	101 7/8	97	94 1/2	22 7/8	21 5/8	106 1/2	101 1/4	.....	.....	.....	.....
1877	98 7/8	93 1/4	88 1/2	81	22 1/4	20 9/16	104 5/8	102 1/4	.....	.....	.....	.....
1880	100	92 15/16	81 3/8	77 3/4	20 3/8	19 3/4	105 5/8	102 1/2	.....	.....	.....	.....
1884	100 5/8	95 5/16	81 3/4	78 1/4	19 3/4	18 15/16	104 3/8	101 5/8	107 1/8	101 3/4	96 1/4	91 1/2
1887	99 3/16	95 5/16	71 11/16	67 7/8	18 3/16	16 5/8	102 3/4	100 1/2	103 1/4	100 1/4	92 5/8	85 3/8
1890	193 7/8	96 13/16	87 1/4	68 3/4	20 29/32	16 7/8	.....	.....	108 1/2	105 1/4	100 3/4	95 1/4
1891	107 13/16	104 1/16	80 3/4	74 1/4	18 1/4	16 5/8	.....	.....	109 1/2	105	99	94 1/2
1892	108 15/16	103 11/16	74 1/2	62	16 11/16	14 5/8	.....	.....	109 1/2	106 1/8	98 1/2	94 7/8

The Indian Government would have had great difficulty also in placing their silver obligations, if they had issued no other kind. For the English investor preferred a less rate of interest to buying a bond with a fluctuating income; and the Indian investment market is far from being sufficiently developed to satisfy the pecuniary needs of the government. A large sum is constantly required especially for railway construction, and hence the sterling debt rose from £68.14 millions in 1881–2 to £107.40 millions in 1891–2. The annual requirements for the permanent national debt are at present about £2.5 to 2.6 millions, and, for the railway debt and for sinking-fund payments on the railways purchased by the state, about £3.5 millions. In addition, there is an item of £2.1 millions for the guaranteed private railways. The service of the public debt, including sinking-funds and payments to the guaranteed lines, therefore, rises to £8.3 millions, or more than half of the demands of the Indian Government in England.

Next to the service of the public debt comes the provisions for pensions; under which there is to be paid in gold for pensions, retirement-payments, etc., for the army ("non-effective army") about £2.2 millions; for the civil administration about £2.0 millions,—or an annual total of about £4.3 millions.

The third large item of gold payments is that stated under "army effective" as about £2.4 millions. The expenditures of especial importance are those for transportation of troops, mobilization, etc.

The other items are of much less importance: for cost of administration in England about one-half million pounds sterling are paid. The remaining expenditures in gold are too insignificant to require mention.

(*b*) TO BE PAID IN SILVER.

It would carry us too far afield to speak here in detail regarding the expenditures to be paid in silver.

But above all, attention should be directed to the army budget; the expenses for the army are exceedingly large. They amounted in recent years to about Rx. 15.6 millions; and if we include the expenses to be paid in England mentioned above, and adding loss by exchange, we reach the large sum of over Rx. 23.5 millions. The strength of the army was, in 1889–90, 72,444 Europeans, 145,363 natives, and 998 officers of various ranks,—or in all 218,805 men. The Indian Army budget is rising slowly, because the cost of maintaining the British troops is yearly becoming dearer. For the pay[1] of British troops stationed in India or in other parts of the British possessions is fixed in sterling, and must be reduced to the standard of the country where the respective troops are serving at a rate to be determined annually and approximating as nearly as possible to the yearly average. In addition, if we include the fact that the obtaining of gold for that part of the army expenses to be paid in England becomes dearer yearly with the fall in the price of silver, there results a rise in the budget from Rx. 20.7 millions (1889–90) to Rx. 23.0 millions (1893–4). The expenditure of 230 millions rupees for the army is no light burden for India, especially if we regard these two things. In the first place a large part of the army is maintained only from the point of view of European politics; because, in case of a conflict between England and Russia, an attack of the latter power on India is feared, and the garrisons in the northwest are strong, much stronger than the

[1] *Financial Statement* for 1893–4, p. 11.

safety of the country would otherwise require;[1] for the eventual invasion of the enemy is to be expected from there. But, secondly, the strength of the Indian Army is partly determined by the fact that Indian troops are for the most part used in the colonial wars of the English, as against Afghanistan, in Egypt, and in South Africa; and consequently a greater effective strength is required.

The Indian debt contracted in silver is likewise very considerable, but, for the reasons above given, it increases much more slowly than the sterling debt. In 1891-2 it amounted to Rx. 102.69 millions as against Rx. 88.65 millions in 1881–2.

The cost of the civil administration is partly borne by the Indian Empire, but partly also by the provinces and local governments. The latter have to meet almost entirely the cost of building roads, of justice, of police, and of schools, and partly of the expenses of collecting the taxes (but excluding a large part of the administration of the land tax). The remaining costs of administration are covered by the Empire. The figures of the budget are as follows:

EXPENSES IN INDIA (INCLUSIVE OF ARMY AND RAILWAYS).

	Expenditures of Empire	Expenses of the Provincial and Local Governments
	Rx.	Rx.
1891–2 definitive	41,296,663	24,708,097
1892–3 revised estimate	41,341.600	23,623,500
1893–4 estimate	42,464,200	24,108,100

Under administration, that for the railways requires only slight aid. The provision for railways is included under interest payments of the railway debt and the transactions with the guaranteed lines:

	Income	Expenditures	Deficit
	Rx.	Rx.	Rx.
1891–2 definitive	19,938,046	20,253,910	315,864
1892–3 revised estimate	19,064,200	20,775,000	1,710,800
1893–4 estimate	19,551,700	21,545,800	1,994,100

[1] It should not be forgotten that the semi-military, organized police amounted in 1891, according to the *Statistical Abstract*, p. 60, to 152,499 men.

The sums are balanced by the surplus of the post office, telegraphs, and mint, which in the three years amounted to Rx. 146,548, 227,100, and 111,500 respectively.

(*c*) THE INCOME.[1]

The chief source of income is the land tax. The results (for the Indian Empire, the provinces, and the local governments combined) were as follows,—or more than one-fourth of the total income of the state :

	Gross, excluding "Refunds and Drawbacks"	Cost of Collection	Net
	Rx.	Rx.	Rx.
1891–2 definitive	23,901,284	3,835,126	20,066,158
1892–3 revised estimate	24,800,500	3,956,100	20,844,400
1893–4 estimate	25,101,200	4,112,300	20,988,900

In India the state or monarch has always had a share of the rent or increment derived from real estate. This tax is levied according to a valuation in which are included estates whether cultivated by the owner or rented. In certain districts, which annually pay about Rx. 4,311,000, the valuation was definitely fixed for all future time about 100 years ago. The remaining parts of India are newly valued at periods of from 10 to 30 years. In the case of large estates of a few hundred up to several thousand acres the share is usually about a half of the rent enjoyed by the owner. In the case of small estates farmed by their owners, the land tax is levied on the cultivated area at a rate determined in each case by the fertility of the soil, and representing about one-half the net product. The districts valued for all time comprise the greater part of Bengal, a quarter of Madras and certain districts in the south of the northwestern provinces. As concerns the portions valued at briefer intervals, the land situated in the northwestern provinces, in Punjab, Oudh, the central provinces and Orissa is held in communal ownership or by large

[1] The statements regarding the tax system are taken, when not otherwise mentioned, from *The Statement exhibiting the Moral and Material Progress and Condition of India*, 1889–90; the tables of figures, as in former quotations, from the *Financial Statement.*

proprietors; while in Bombay, Burma, Assam and Berar, as well as in the greater part of Madras, the land is cultivated by small proprietors. In the districts valued for the indefinite future the land tax amounts to about two-thirds of a rupee per acre of cultivated land, and represents about one-fifth of the net product, or about one-twenty-fourth of the gross product. On the average the natural advantages of climate and of soil are greater here than in the districts revalued periodically. In the latter the land tax amounts to about one and one-half rupees per acre of cultivated land, which is somewhat less than one-half of the actual or estimated net product, and probably one-tenth or one-twelfth of the gross product. The figures of the net product and the land tax vary greatly according to the fertility of the soil, the climate, the rainfall and the possibility of bringing the produce to market or to the seacoast. Payment for water which is delivered by the state canal, or reservoirs, for the purpose of irrigation is regulated either according to the extent of the area irrigated or of the water used. If a land owner or a tenant undertakes improvements he is not thereby more heavily mulcted by the land tax.[1]

That so unusually heavy a tax—at least to the European mind—can be increased only with difficulty is clear without further explanation. Besides, the Indian farmer is in such a pitiful material condition, he groans so heavily under excessive exactions both from the landlord and the usurer, that an increase of the land-tax would easily entirely annihilate him. In their own interest the English dare not act like Asiatic conquerors who squeeze the last drop of blood out of the people and wholly ruin them without compunction in order to enrich themselves.

Next in importance to the land-tax comes the tax on salt

[1] Details on the land tax are given by: Wolf, *Thatsachen und Aussichten der Ostindischen Konkurrenz im Weizenhandel*, p. 52 *et seq.*; Ruhland, *Aus dem Verfassungs- und Verwaltungsrecht des Britisch-indischen Kaiserreiches*, p. 408; Hunter, *The Indian Empire*, p. 333 *et seq.* The latter gives much lower figures than the official report above cited. According to him, the officers entrusted with the collection of the land tax make so many deductions in favor of the farmer that the tax on the average amounts to only 5.50 per centum of the gross product.

which yields a yearly net of about Rx. 8.1 millions. It is levied either as an import-duty upon all salt imported, or as a tax upon that produced in India. Its rate fluctuated formerly from one-fifth rupee in Burma to three and one-fourth rupees in Bengal for a maund of 82 lbs. In 1889–90, it amounted to two and one-half rupees in the whole of India except in Burma where only one rupee was levied. It is also very difficult to increase the salt tax, because the poorest people are heavily burdened by it.

Opium brings in not much less than salt; although in this case the tax does not fall on the Indians, but on the Chinese; since it is levied only on the opium transported to China, and this has almost no competition. The returns from it, exclusive of the very considerable cost of collection, are from Rx. 5 to 6.5 millions. The results vary largely, because they depend upon the condition of the market and upon the fate of the crops. The opium tax is levied partly through a monopoly in Bengal, partly through the duty upon all opium exported from the native states.

Although the poppy grows wild over the largest part of India, its cultivation on British soil is permitted only in parts of Bengal, the northwestern provinces and Oudh. A few thousand acres in Punjab are cultivated for local use. The opium-farmer in the monopoly districts receives aid which enables him to prepare the soil for the crop. He then has to deliver the whole product to an opium-agent at a fixed price, through whom it passes to the state factory at Patna and Ghazipur where it is then prepared for the Chinese market. The boxes of prepared opium are disposed of at monthly auctions in Calcutta; to prevent speculation and to keep the price steady the quantity of opium to be offered for sale at each auction is published a year beforehand. In 1892–3, 48,850 boxes were sold at an average of 1247 rupees per box, while the estimate had assumed only 1050 rupees. For 1893–4 an average price of 1250 rupees is anticipated, although less will be brought to sale on account of a poor crop.

In many native states of Rajputana and of Central India opium is likewise cultivated. These states have entered into contracts with the Anglo-Indian government in which they bind themselves to adapt their own to the British system and to prevent smuggling. Upon all the opium which is exported from their territory for the Chinese market they raise a considerable tax, and this opium pays into the Indian tax collectors a return which a few years ago was lowered from Rs. 650 to Rs. 600 a box. An increase of the income from opium does not depend upon the Indian Government but upon the outcome of the crop.

The next important source of income is the excise, which yields a net of Rx. 4.9 to Rx. 5.0 millions. This is partly levied by granting a monopoly of the sale of spirituous liquors and poisonous drugs to a county (*Bezirk*), and, partly, the sale of these articles is permitted only to the possessor of a license. In several regions also a brandy tax is levied according to the percentage of alcohol in the product.[1] The excise does not seem capable of increase, because for the most part the tribes addicted to drink live in forests and mountains difficult to watch, and in these sparsely settled regions the material for illicit distillation is easily obtained.

Tobacco, sugar, tea and coffee are untaxed; they grow throughout all India and are consumed by all classes of people. Tobacco is cultivated in almost every village, and old and young, man and woman, smoke. Regarding the possibility of a tax on tobacco and sugar, the report of the Herschell Committee says, § 42: "To procure a revenue from them by means of taxation would involve constant and vexatious interference with the people, and the cost of collecting and enforcing the tax would be enormous in proportion to the sum realized. Those who have given evidence on this subject, and who entertain the gravest objections to an increase of the salt tax, are nevertheless of opinion that, with all its evils, this would be preferable to an attempt to raise a revenue by a taxation of sugar or tobacco."

[1] For details see *Statement Exhibiting the Moral and Material Progress and Condition of India*, 1889–90, p. 90; and Ruhland, *loc. cit.*, p. 442.

The income from stamps is very considerable. The returns from them are rapidly rising. In 1861–2 they amounted to Rx. 1.7 millions; today they are nearly Rx. 4.3 millions. The stamp duties are levied according to Act VII. of 1870 (Court Fees Act) which lays a tax on complaints, petitions and other documents to be brought before the civil, criminal and revenue courts; and also according to Act I. of 1879 (Stamp Act) taxes are laid upon papers required in trade, such as bills of lading, evidences of debt, checks, bills of exchange, quittances, etc. The tax collected from the dealings of private persons with the public authorities constitutes two-thirds of the income from stamps.

There exists, besides, an income tax, according to Act II. of 1886. All incomes arising from salaries, pensions and interest on investments, if they amount to more than Rs. 2000 annually, pay five pie per rupee (2.6 per cent.); if below Rs. 2000, four pie per rupee (2 per cent.). Companies have to pay five pie on each rupee of their net income. Every income from other sources pays a tax according to a scale, which rises progressively from Rs. 10 on Rs. 500 to Rs. 42 on Rs. 1999. The tax on incomes over Rs. 2000 is, as in the first case, five pie per rupee. All annual incomes under Rs. 500 are untaxed, as are also all those arising from agriculture, and the salaries of military men, provided they are less than Rs. 500 per month. This tax yields something over Rx. 1.6 millions.

The introduction of an income tax was regarded with very great dissatisfaction by the European officials of the government, because they had been seriously injured besides this by the fall in the rate of exchange, and they rather expected an alleviation than an addition to their burden. And yet the income tax is the necessary completion of the existing system of taxation. Agriculture is heavily burdened by the land-tax, and it is not more than right and just that the incomes from commerce and industry, which are exceptionally large in India, and which would be wholly exempt without the income tax, should also contribute something to the burdens of the state. That the officials, whose salaries are quite exactly known, should be most seriously affected by this tax is in the nature of things, in a country like India.

The customs duties have so far brought in relatively small returns—only about Rx. 1.50 millions—because India has had nearly complete free trade. Of the import duties only that on spirituous liquors is moderately profitable; it yielded, in 1891–2, Rx. 589,684. There exists, further, an import duty of six pie per gallon on petroleum and other mineral oils. The import duty on salt has already been spoken of under the salt tax, and is also presented there in the Indian budget. A tax of no financial gain, but one extremely characteristic in the ways and means of Anglo-Indian colonial policy, is that on weapons and munitions, which ranks third among existing import duties. It is almost prohibitive: guns pay, *e. g.*, Rs. 50, pistols Rs. 15. But persons who have weapon permits pay only 10 per cent. ad valorem on weapons destined for their own use. This duty on weapons may have contributed not a little to the result that the quiet and safety of the country is today so marked. Of the system of export duties so fully elaborated by the Mohammedans in earlier times there now exists only an export duty on rice, of three annas per Indian maund of $82\frac{2}{7}$ pounds, whose amount varies with the outcome of the crop.

The remaining income from forests, tributes of the feudal states, etc., are small.

The total income of the Empire from taxes and duties amounts to:

1891–2 definitive - - - - - - - Rx. 49,969,887
1892–3 revised estimate - - - - - " 51,473,400
1893–4 estimate - - - - - - - - " 50,103,200

The provinces and local governments, to cover their expenditures, raise sums in addition to the land-tax and stamp-duties, and also their own provincial taxes, which are placed at:

1891–2 definitive - - - - - - - Rx. 24,467,173
1892–3 revised estimate - - - - - " 23,259,700
1893–4 estimate - - - - - - - - " 23,356,900

If the income from railways, as given above, is counted in

here, and also the smaller returns from waterworks, etc., the total of the income amounts to:

1891–2 definitive - - - - - - -	Rx. 89,143,283
1892–3 revised estimate - - - - -	" 90,021,200
1893–4 estimate - - - - - - - -	" 90,005,700

If we set off the expenditures of:

1891–2 definitive - - - - - - -	Rx. 88,675,748
1892–3 revised estimate - - - - -	" 91,103,100
1893–4 estimate - - - - - - - -	" 91,600,800

there results:

1891–2 a surplus of - - - - - -	Rx. 467,535
1892–3 a deficit of - - - - - -	" 1,081,900
1893–4 a deficit of - - - - - -	" 1,595,100

(*d*) CRITICISM.

To recapitulate briefly, the Indian budget shows a slow but steady increase of income, and, also, of the expenditures to be disbursed in silver. But the ultimate condition of the finances is dependent upon the rate of exchange; with each decline of the rate there is an increase in the total of exchange, computed, of course, in rupees, which the Indian Government must sell in London. The unfortunate thing is that a great part of their expenses are payable in gold, while all the income is paid in silver.

In the present depressed conditions of the rates of exchange the situation of the Indian Government has become decidedly critical. The amounts which are needed to meet their gold demands have become, owing to the renewed decline in the rates of exchange, even much greater than was expected by Sir David Barbour in his very pessimistic estimate for 1893–4; and the deficit will accordingly be considerably greater. In order that this deficit should not become chronic, the means of relief adopted must be drastic. This is only possible either by a reduction of expenditures, or by an increase of income. But, as matters now stand, any material saving can be carried through only in connection with the army. Since the Indian Army, as is unanimously agreed by all those conversant with the condition of affairs, is probably now only barely competent to meet any Russian attack, and since an increase of the present effective would be very desirable for the integrity of the British Empire, therefore a saving here for India would only be possible if England should assume a part of the cost of defending the Empire, as is also done in other colonies. But this is not to be thought of at present; for any English Government would be on its guard against offering to its constituents new taxes in favor of India.

There remains, therefore, only an increase of the income. But, since all the Indian experts agree in urging that an increase of the taxes already existing is fraught with great economic and political danger, the proposal recently made to impose a customs-duty on cotton goods ought to have deserved some attention. Very many things in the actual situation favor such a duty. Above all, the financial condition of the government, as we saw above, is extremely precarious. As the value of cotton manufactures annually imported is about Rs. 300 millions, such a duty would be financially very profitable. Furthermore, it might be of some assistance to the cotton industry of the country which has been seriously injured by the late currency reform, by being cut off from East Asia, its principal foreign market. Lancashire possesses in East Asia a signal advantage over India; because, in trading with countries possessing different monetary standards—and now India has one kind, while China, Japan, etc., have another kind—the essential basis is an admirable organization of currency and banking. In this respect, the English cotton industry, supported by the greatest money market in the world, has an indefinite advantage over India. It might go hard with the Indian cotton spinners under the changed conditions to maintain the East Asian market, which was won with difficulty, against the competition of the English, and also that of the Chinese and Japanese which has lately appeared. The Indian cotton industry is now more than ever dependent on the home market, and hence, from the Indian standpoint, a duty upon imported fabrics would certainly be of advantage. Lancashire, too, could bear such a duty fairly well, because, as said, it has obtained a more than sufficient compensation through the currency reform, through the greater steadiness of the rates of exchange between England and India conditioned on a more reasonable policy of the Indian Government, and through the advantage it possesses in the East Asian markets. However, another way out of the difficulty has meanwhile been adopted. A duty on cotton goods was avoided; and instead of it, in March, 1894, a 5 per centum ad valorem duty was imposed on all other articles of importation, including silver. The English interests overcame the Indian.

II. THE COMPLAINTS OF OFFICIALS.

If we take into account the fact that a thorough-going increase of salaries for the European officials of the Government cannot be postponed, the question of financial reform, or the obtaining a higher income, becomes of especial importance. For years there has prevailed among the Indian officials a deep-seated dissatisfaction in consequence of the difficulties arising from the fall in the rate of exchange; and J. T. Wheeler, sometime Professor of Moral Philosophy and Logic at Madras College, as the representative of the "Indian Uncovenanted Civil Servants," reproached the Indian Government before the Gold and Silver Commission[1] with insisting on their bond, like Shylock, if they do not raise the salaries of officials. The condition of the Indian officials is best reflected in an address[2] by Mr. D. R. Lyall, on the occasion of the reception of a deputation of high Indian officials by the viceroy, Lord Landsdowne, on January 31, 1893, as follows:

"This disastrous fall in the value of the currency in which the officers of the Indian Government are paid has affected all branches of the Service alike. For, although the conditions of service are different in different branches, and all have not suffered in precisely the same manner or in the same degree, yet the differences are insignificant in comparison with the losses which

[1] Question 2217.

[2] *Minutes of Evidence, Indian Currency Committee*, p. 186.

all have suffered in common. Since 1886, when the depreciation of silver became acute, there has been a sharp and rapid rise in the price of almost all articles produced in India, including food, in the wages of servants, and in house rent. In the same period the retail price of goods imported from Europe, on which a portion of our salaries is spent, has also risen largely from the same cause; and the prices paid for them increase with each successive fall in exchange.

"We do not, however, desire to dwell at length on this part of the case. We mention it in order to show that the fall in the value of silver seriously affects us, even in our expenditure in India. What we wish to press most earnestly upon your Excellency's attention is the cruel and intolerable burden which has been laid upon us in respect of that portion of our expenditure which has to be incurred at home. Your Excellency is doubtless aware that, if a European officer, whether soldier or civilian, is to render efficient service to Government in a tropical climate, it is necessary for him to take leave periodically to England to recruit his health. If he has to give his children an education of the same stamp as he has himself received, he must send them to England to school. If he is to lay by a little money as an addition to his pension after retirement, or as a provision for his widow and others dependent on him after his death, he must be enabled to remit it to the country in which it will be spent. All these are as much the just and reasonable necessities of his position as the ability to provide himself with food and clothing from day to day. Yet it is the literal truth that, under present conditions, these moderate and reasonable requirements are beyond the reach of many, if not most of your Excellency's European officers, and are becoming increasingly difficult for all.

"We will not weary your Excellency with a long list of actual instances. A single typical case will suffice. We will take the case of an officer whose pay is Rs. 800 a month, and who has a wife and two or three children to support at home. That sum represents the pay of a Senior Chaplain, of a second grade District Superintendent of Police, and of a second grade Sub-Deputy

Opium Agent; and we would explain that, on the Bengal establishment, the average length of service of the officers now in those grades is 16 years, 29 years, and 28 years respectively.

"Such an officer's remittances to his family cannot, at a low estimate, be placed at less than £400 a year if his children are of an age requiring education. At the present rate of exchange, that sum costs him more than Rs. 6,500, thus leaving him Rs. 258 a month for subsistence. After deduction of fund subscriptions and income-tax, he is left with less than Rs. 200 a month to live on. Even in the case of men who have been fortunate in their promotion, or who are members of a higher paid branch of the service, and who receive pay of Rs. 1000 a month, the sum left for subsistence in India would amount to less than Rs. 400 a month, after deductions as above. It is evident that such men cannot save; in fact, it is difficult for them to keep clear of debt. The case is still worse if the Government servant falls ill, or is for other reasons compelled to take leave. His maximum furlough pay is then Rs. 6000 a year, which at the present rate of exchange gives him only £367 a year on which to maintain himself and his family and educate his children. It is manifest that the prospect of having to subsist on such an allowance goes far towards neutralizing the value of the furlough rules in the case of European officers.

"But in the Indian Staff Corps, and in most of the large Civil Departments in India, an officer of from 15 to 20 years' service seldom draws so much as Rs. 800 to Rs. 1000 a month. After twenty years' service an officer of the Staff Corps attains the rank of Major, and receives, with allowances, about Rs. 900 per month, while as a Captain his pay up to the completion of his twentieth year is, with allowances, less than Rs. 600 per mensem. In the Public Works Department the rank of Executive Engineer, second grade, which is reached in about seventeen years' service, carries a pay of Rs. 800 per month. In the other principal European departments, officers of from 15 to 20 years service are commonly in receipt of salaries not exceeding Rs. 600 to Rs. 800 per month. The condition of these services is being subjected to a complete revolution in consequence of the fall in exchange. Hitherto, an officer entering the Staff Corps, or one of the great Civil Departments, expected to retain his connection with his own country. He expected to be able to send his children home to be suitably educated; to take furlough to England from time to time for the sake of his health, and also to visit his relatives and family; and, finally, to save a part of his pay, which, added to his pension, would enable him to live in comparative comfort after his retirement. These just and reasonable expectations are now defeated. It is now utterly impossible for many officers, even those who have been fortunate in their promotion, to afford the expense of educating their children at home. Every year men are being driven in increasing numbers to send their sons and daughters to hill schools, to deny themselves and their wives the advantage of a periodical visit to their own country, and to relinquish all expectation of saving a little money to eke out their pensions when they retire. Year by year it is becoming plain that a larger and larger proportion of the men who accept Government service in India must abandon the hope of ever returning home. They must be content to settle permanently in India; while their children, receiving an inferior education and brought up amid un-English surroundings, sink to a lower social level, and swell the mass of the unemployed white population, whose growth is already a source of grave anxiety.

"It is impossible to look for the indefinite continuance of faithful and contented work, when the workers are placed in a position of anxiety and embarrassment deepening into despondency. There is happily as yet little cause to fear that any of those whom we represent may be led to fall away from the high standing of which both the Indian Government and its servants are justly proud. But your Excellency will, we are assured, be alive to the necessity of placing even the humblest of your European officers byond the reach of temptation. And as it becomes more generally known that, to the disadvantages inseparable from an Indian career, there must now be added the prospect of poverty so great as to involve the possible severance of home ties, it can scarcely be doubted that Her Majesty's Secretary of State will find it increasingly difficult to obtain fresh recruits for the Indian Services of the same stamp as at present.

"Officers of the Civil Service and the Staff Corps are now beginning to find that their pensions after retirement, which are fixed in sterling, are worth almost as much as their salaries during active service, which are payable in rupees. These officers have thus every inducement to retire as soon as they have completed the minimum periods of service required by the rules, thereby prematurely swelling the pension list, and impairing the efficiency of the public service by the early withdrawal of experienced officers still capable of active work. . . .

"We pray your Excellency to take these matters into your favorable consideration, and secure for us such an adjustment of our salaries, as will make them not less valuable to us than they were intended to be when they were fixed. In Ceylon, we understand that the pay of the civil servants of the Colony was fixed several years ago at the rate of 1s. 10½d. to the rupee. We do not wish to define the precise form in which similar assistance might most suitably be granted to Her Majesty's Indian servants; but would beg your Excellency to believe that we have not exaggerated our distress, and to grant to us the fullest measure of relief, in such manner as your Excellency's advisers may think fit."

Lord Roberts, the commander-in-chief of the Indian Army, expressed himself to the same effect as Mr. Lyall, in a memorandum[1] addressed to the viceroy on the occasion of the reception of the above-mentioned deputation, on the hardships to the Indian officials arising from the fall in the rate of exchange.

The question of raising the salaries of officers also has a very grave political side. No one goes for pleasure alone into the fever districts of Lower Bengal, or into the deserts of Rajputana as a revenue officer, or as a judge; if a highly tempting salary is not offered, the government simply finds no one fit for the posts. To the present time, the services of the Anglo-Indian adminis-

[1] Appendix to *Minutes of Evidence, Indian Currency Committee*, p. 189.

tration have been unmistakably brilliant. The country is admirably governed. "There is no other country in the world which, under equally difficult conditions, would be governed equally well."[1] Although only 100 years ago fire and sword, destruction and war were the order of the day, there now reigns throughout the length and breadth of the empire, from Cape Comorin to the snow-bound peaks of the Himalayas, from the boundaries of Afghanistan to the coast of Coromandel, the *pax britannica*, the most profound peace. Justice prevails everywhere, and the country is developing economically in a decidedly wonderful manner. Everywhere, the English official in India to the present day stands as the model of honesty and integrity and the possessor of an admirable tact. And, for pecuniary considerations should the government invite the risk of this becoming otherwise? No,—it is of vital interest to the country that the integrity of the officials should be protected by a sufficient compensation. Should it be otherwise, that would be the beginning of the end.

[1] Ruhland, *loc. cit.*, p. 224.

CHAPTER IV.

HISTORY OF THE INDIAN SILVER CURRENCY.

I. THE EARLIER TIMES TO 1835.

Silver, gold, and copper were the metals used in the earliest Indian monetary system; and, as was universal in the beginning, when metallic money was adopted the fine metal was weighed out in payments.[1] The unit of weight was the *rati*, of 1.75 grains troy, whose weight was equivalent to that of the seed of the*a brus precatorius;* 100 ratis formed the *sata-raktika* in common use; and this weight of money can not only be traced back to the time of the Vedas, but it also formed the basis for the development of the modern British rupee.

Silver was from the beginning the money-metal most in use in India, although gold, especially in the south, played no unimportant rôle. For this reason we intend to treat of the silver money first.

A. THE SILVER MONEY.

Sher Shah chose the above mentioned money-weight of 100 ratis, in 1542, as a basis, when he coined his *rupyam* (silver coin) containing about 176 grains of silver. Many local rupees followed this first one, all different in weight and fineness. The first English rupee was the "rupee of Bombay," in the year 1677, weighing 167.8 grains. In 1600, Queen Elizabeth had caused "portcullis pieces of eight" to be coined, in order that her face should be as highly esteemed in distant Asia as that of the Spanish king. By 1758, before the British power was permanently established, English rupees were coined in only limited quanti-

[1] The statements to p. 85 are almost entirely borrowed from Chalmers, *History of Currency in the British Colonies*, p. 336. See, further, Laughlin, "Indian Monetary History," and Molesworth, *Indian Currency*.

ties. Before 1835 there were three principal kinds of rupees, the sicca-rupee in Bengal, the surat-rupee in Bombay, and the arcot-rupee in Madras.

(a) From 1773 on, in order to prevent the clipping by the money-changers, the *sicca-rupee* of Bengal was provided with an inscription "19 San Sikkah" (*i. e.*, coined in the 19th year of Shah Alam, the last of the Moguls). This coin containing in gross weight about 180 grains and of fine silver about 176 grains, remained in circulation, with slight change, until their coinage was stopped by Act XIII. of 1836. Since January 1, 1838, the sicca-rupee has not been a legal means of payment.

(b) The old *Bombay rupee* was somewhat lighter than the sicca-rupee, although containing more fine silver. The *surat-rupee* of the natives was intended to be of like weight and fineness. But, since it was coined of less value, it drove the English coins out of circulation; hence in the last twenty years of the preceding century none of the Bombay rupees were coined. In 1881 a new Bombay rupee was ordered to be coined of 179 grains gross weight and about 165 grains fine weight, or about the present proportion. In 1824 Bombay adopted the coinage system of Madras.

(c) Before 1818 the *arcot-rupee* of Madras, which was struck at the mint of Fort St. George, contained 166.477 grains of fine silver. Because the gold was valued too highly as compared with silver, and because of the coinage of a domestic arcot-rupee of less value, the silver rupee could have but little importance in comparison with the gold *pagoda* and *fanam*,[1] a small native silver coin rated higher than the British rupee.

In 1806, it was ordered by England that the current coin of Madras should be a silver rupee of a gross weight of 180 grains, $\frac{11}{12}$ fine, and so containing 165 grains fine silver. But the new coin was not introduced until a proclamation was issued January 7, 1818; and 350 rupees were to equal 100 pagodas.

(d) Although the Company intended to introduce a uniform coinage, as early as 1806, into all their Asiatic possessions, this

[1] *Fanam* is probably the Arabian expression for the Tamil word, *panam* (money).

purpose was not effected until a generation later. By 1806, under the influence of Lord Liverpool's *Letter to the King*, they had, as is distinctly admitted, decided upon monometalism; and only silver could be the money metal. But it was only by Act XVII. of 1835, that a uniform silver rupee, and the corresponding pieces of half-rupees, were introduced throughout all India as the legal means of payment. The type chosen for the new company rupee was the Madras rupee of 1818, containing 180 grains troy of gross weight and 165 grains of fine silver; it was, as stated above, introduced into Bombay in 1824. Since 1862 the rupee has been provided with the effigy of the Queen instead of the escutcheon of the East India Company; and since then it is called "the Government rupee."

B. GOLD.

(*a*) THE MOHUR.

Like the silver rupee, the gold mohur (Persian *muhr* means seal) has the old Indian weight of 100 ratis, or 175 grains fine gold. In the fourteenth century a mohur of about 300 grains was coined for a time,—apparently in order to approximate to the then existing relation between silver and gold, but they later returned to the old weight of the *sata-raktika*. After 1758 the East India Company endeavored to make gold the monetary standard in India.

"Under the native governments" (Ordinance XXXV. of Bengal in 1793), "and until the year 1766, the gold mohur was not adopted as a legal means of payment in public or private obligations, nor had the government fixed the number of rupees to which it was to be equal. It was only coined for the convenience of certain individuals, and its market price was affected by fluctuations like those of other goods, for silver was the common measure of value throughout the country. In 1766 the gold mohur was declared to be a legal means of payment; it was to be equal to 14 sicca-rupees. This, however, did not correspond to the market ratio; hence in 1769 the value of the gold mohur was fixed at 16 sicca-rupees. This was another error.

In Bombay it was ordained, in 1774, that a gold mohur should be struck of the weight of the silver rupee and of the fineness of the Venetian *zecchino*; hence the ratio was about 1:15. When the surat-rupee came into circulation the ratio was changed to 1:13. In order to obtain relief, it was enacted in 1800 that the gold mohur should have the same gross and fine weight as the silver rupee, and should be equivalent to 15 silver rupees.

Ordinance XLV. of Bengal, in 1803, expressly declared the gold mohur to be the money of trade. In 1806, when they were discussing the introduction of a uniform standard in India, the coinage of a gold rupee of 180 grains troy gross weight and 165 grains fine weight was proposed. This was done, in 1818, in Madras, where the gold rupee was received and paid out at all public treasuries "at a rate fixed by a proclamation of the government. The present ratio of one gold rupee for 15 silver rupees shall continue until changed by a new proclamation." In Bengal, Ordinance XIV., of 1818, decreed that the gold mohur, reduced to a fineness of 22 carats, should be worth 16 silver rupees.

When the principles of 1806 were adopted in India in the year 1835, Act XVII. of that year said: "That no gold coins shall henceforth be a legal means of payment in any of the possessions of the East India Company."

(*b*) THE PAGODA.

The gold coin of southern India is a native *varāha* or *hūn*. The first name means the boar of Vishnu, which has been stamped on the coins of southern India since the fifth or sixth century under the Chalukya dynasty; *hūn* (gold) is the later Mahommedan name. From the sixteenth century on, if not somewhat earlier, the Portuguese gave to this coin the name of *pardao de ouro*.

In Madras, before 1818, the current coin was a star-pagoda,—its device being a star; it contained 42.048 grains of fine gold and was worth 7s. 5¼d. This pagoda, as well as some other

South-Indian gold coins of like name (the Pondicherry and and Porto-Novo pagodas) which differ but slightly from the Madras pagoda, were used in Ceylon and Mauritius, and even at the Cape of Good Hope and St. Helena. In 1800 the pagoda was declared a legal tender in New South Wales.

In 1806, when the directors of the East India Company were discussing the reform of the Indian monetary system and decided upon the silver standard, it was then felt that some modifications were necessary "in Madras, where gold is the principal money in circulation and the money of account, and in which the troops are mostly paid. Not in the least is it our wish to introduce a silver standard to the exclusion of gold, where the latter is the common measure of value."

In 1810 the minting of gold coins was restricted; their paying power was likewise limited. By proclamation of January 7, 1818, the new silver rupee was introduced as the legal means of payment in the Presidency and the coinage of pagodas stopped; instead of that, as above mentioned, the coinage of a gold rupee was ordered, and its equivalent in silver at the treasury was given.

II. ATTEMPTS AT REFORM SINCE 1835.

We saw that, in 1835, the simple silver standard was introduced into British East-India. Soon after that, however, attempts were begun to again make a place for gold in the Indian coinage system. The first step was taken in the proclamation of January 13, 1841, in which the public treasuries were instructed to receive the gold mohur in payment for 15 rupees. The gold mohurs, whose coinage was by Act XVII. of 1835 thenceforth permitted, thereby became a legal payment at the treasury. Yet almost no gold was coined; and although the charge for seigniorage was lowered, by 1847 there was scarcely any gold in circulation. When the Californian and Australian gold discoveries came, a depreciation of gold began to be feared, and hence, by ordinance of December 22, 1852, the right to pay gold coins at the treasuries was withdrawn from January 1, 1853.

But when, in the beginning of the sixties, in consequence of the "cotton famine"; the importation of the precious metals to India rose enormously, the Chambers of Commerce of Bombay and Madras believed the time had arrived to begin an energetic agitation in favor of introducing the gold standard. While the Chamber of Madras, however, in its address to the viceroy of April 30, 1864, limited itself to pointing out the inconveniences occasioned to merchants by large payments in silver—since the adoption of paper money had made no progress—their colleagues in Bombay were more plain-spoken. It is both entertaining and interesting to read the address[1] of this Chamber on the eighth and nineteenth of February 1864.

In a report it is said "that the exclusion of gold from our currency cannot be justified, and that this must be regarded simply as barbarous, irrational and unnatural." They argued that from time immemorial India had possessed a gold standard until the coinage law of 1835 had robbed gold of its property as a legal means of payment. But gold could not thereby have lost its popularity; on the contrary gold coins are still much sought for, and a high premium is paid for them. The report goes on to say "that the continued movement of silver to India must bring disturbance, if not destruction, to the silver standards of all other nations, and that it is to the interest of India as well as of all the rest of the world, that the movement which causes this exhaustion should be removed by the introduction of a gold standard." The chamber moved in favor of appointing a commission. Their resolutions were warmly supported by the governor of Bombay in a report dated February 23, 1864. Then on November 23, 1864, legal tender power at the treasury was granted to the English sovereign at the rate of 10 rupees and to the half-sovereign for 5 rupees.

The desire for a gold currency, to which the Chamber of Commerce at Calcutta gave renewed expression, led to the appointment of the Mansfield Commission[2] which reported on

[1] *Papers relating to a Gold Currency for India*, 1864, pp. 5 and 7.

[2] Chalmers, *loc. cit.*, p. 344. J. L. Laughlin, *loc. cit.*, 593. *Report from the Royal Commission on International Coinage*, London, 1868. Questions 297 *et seq.*

October 4, 1866, on the monetary system of India, and recommended the use of gold as a legal means of payment, making the gold mohur worth 15 rupees. Thereupon the Government proclaimed that it was intended to receive the British sovereign at the public offices at the rate of 10 rupees 4 annas. The change in the relative values of the two metals, however, which followed a few years after, did not permit this ordinance to be of any practical value.

But when the depreciation of silver began, and when with it the rate of exchange fell, the Indian Government, being now obliged to furnish more and more silver to meet their gold obligations, came to feel the new hardships in the most unpleasant manner. Hence, in 1878, Lord Lytton submitted propositions to the British Government looking to an increase of the rate of exchange from 1s. 7d. to 2s., by a limitation of the coinage and by an addition to the mint value of the rupee, thereby establishing a fixed ratio between gold and the coined silver rupees. The British Government abruptly declined this proposition.

At the Paris Monetary Conference of 1881, the Indian Government was represented by two bimetallists, Lord Reay and Sir Louis Mallet. At this conference, however, as is well known, nothing was accomplished.

Meanwhile the financial condition of the Indian Government became more and more troublesome. In its despatch of February 2, 1886, the Council of the viceroy, represented to the Secretary of State for India, then Lord Randolph Churchill, the extraordinary importance an international regulation of silver would have for India. Before that, on January 26, the India Office had addressed a letter to the Lord Commissioners of the Treasury, saying: The Secretary of State cannot hesitate to affirm "that there is an urgent necessity for making every possible effort to find a means of freeing the Indian Government from their present condition; and that a comparative steadiness in the relative values of gold and silver would be important for the regular movement of trade, yea, even of most vital interest to India." The Treasury Office answered, under date of May 31, 1886, the despatch of the Indian Government and the letter of the India Office, that they could adopt no measures to promote a monetary conference and take part therein before a policy was adopted which they could follow and approve of; especially, as the whole question is being considered by the Royal Commission on the Depression of Trade and Industry; and, finally, nothing exists which could induce the Lords Commissioners of the Treasury to deviate from the instructions given to the representative of England at the Monetary Conference of 1881. These were to the effect that the English delegate should simply attend the discussions, in order to make communications and furnish information which the Conference might require, but he should have no permission to vote.

The liberal successor to Lord Randolph Churchill did not continue the discussion with the Treasury Office. In the meanwhile, the Tories again came into power, and in September 1886 a Royal Commission was again appointed for the investigation of the recent changes in the relative values of the precious metals (Gold and Silver Commission). The Indian Government under Lord Dufferin laid before this commission a scheme worked out in detail,[1] requiring the double standard for both England and India. The ratio to be chosen should not be less than the average price of both the precious metals in the markets of the world during recent years, and not more favorable for silver than 1:15½. The Gold and Silver Commission, however, resulted in no success; and, for Indian interests, no step was taken.

The price of silver continued to fall steadily. The sudden and striking rise in consequence of the American silver experiment in the year 1890 was only a short interruption. Worse and worse became the condition of the government and of all the interests injured by the decline of silver.

At the end of January, 1892, came the news that the United States of North America intended to invite the other powers to a new monetary conference. Thereupon the Chamber of Commerce of Bombay, in two communications to the Indian Govern-

[1] Appendix XII., *First Report of the Gold and Silver Commission.*

ment on February 4 and 18, pointed out how absolutely necessary it is for India that the international double-standard should be determined upon at the forthcoming conference, and then fully carried out; but that, if no understanding should be reached on this point, the introduction of the gold standard should be taken into serious consideration. The Indian Government transmitted these communications to the Secretary of State, and also pointed out the extremely dangerous effect on India of the expected suspension of silver purchases by the United States.

Upon the announcement that Great Britain had accepted the invitation to the conference, yet that it would not discuss international bimetallism, but only the more extended use of silver for purposes of money, the Indian Government decided to recommend that, in case a direct agreement between the United States and India was not feasible, the Indian mints should be closed to the free coinage of silver, although the government itself should retain the right to coin. If they had foreseen what effect the closing of the mints has had on the gold value of the rupee, they should have opened the mints to the free coinage of gold; the establishment of a ratio between the gold and the silver rupee might have been reserved for further deliberation. The best ratio would probably be, that which corresponded to the market conditions during a limited period before the introduction of the limping gold standard. At the same time, the Minister of Finance, Sir D. M. Barbour, transmitted to the India Office a detailed statement which is of the highest importance. It forms the basis of all the discussions concerning Indian currency affairs to the time of the closing of the mints, and we are probably right in supposing that, so far as conditions allow, it is to be decisive for the future policy of the Indian Government.

We shall reprint the statement verbatim in the appendix. A brief reference to it here is sufficient. Sir David first remarks that, although the proposal aims to stop the free coinage of silver and introduce the gold standard, there is no intention to put gold in the place of silver in the ordinary circulation of the country. For, in the great majority of Indian transactions, silver must remain the medium of exchange. He relies on the example of France and other nations to show that a limping gold standard with a very extended use of overvalued silver coins can very well be maintained. He emphasizes that, in order to make the limping gold standard effective, it is necessary to limit the quantity of these silver coins. These silver coins must be exchangeable at any time for gold coins, either on the payment of a slight premium, or without it. As a rule it is to be expected that gold would be required for silver coins only when gold is wanted for hoards, for export, or for melting. A possibility of accomplishing this purpose, in his opinion, exists in gathering a supply of gold; then—when enough gold is on hand—in opening the mints to the free coinage of gold, in making this metal thereafter legal tender, and in guaranteeing, by the gold reserve collected, the exchangeability of silver and gold coins at their face value.[1] This, however, would be a very costly plan, and there exists the great danger that the whole supply of gold would disappear in exchange for silver coins. For this reason, Sir David Barbour did not recommend this plan, but the one mentioned above, which the Government has made its own. If this last plan should be carried out, and the Government treasury be instructed to exchange gold coins for silver rupees, as soon as such an order was possible, then no premium of any amount whatever on gold coins could exist, so long as the reserves should be maintained in the public treasuries or in that behind the paper money; and the limping gold standard would remain absolutely intact.

After carrying out the proposed measures, it might be possible that no gold would be brought to the mint or put in circulation, and that the value of the rupee should fall below 1s. 4d.—accepting this as the established relation,—or that gold would be brought to be coined only so long as the rupee should be worth 1s. 4d.; but that this then might cease, and the value of the rupee would fall. This would then be a sign that too many silver rupees were in circulation, and that the limping gold

[1] English "face value" means the number of rupees stated on the face of the gold coins.

standard would no longer remain intact. The remedy in such a case would be to limit the circulation of rupees and take measures to improve the general financial condition of the country. Such an improvement would give heightened confidence; and the reduction in the quantity of rupees in circulation, if carried far enough, would finally raise the value of these coins. The greatest danger would probably arise, immediately after the first introduction of the limping gold standard, from the rupees which would return to India from abroad, and from those which would be drawn from hoards and be put into circulation; although Mr. Barbour believes that the hoards would in reality remain practically undisturbed. The limitation of the rupees in circulation would not necessarily be an expensive measure; it could be extended over a series of years. But until it was carried out to a sufficient extent, the limping gold standard could not be introduced. It might be hoped, however, that during the transition period the rate of exchange between England and India would become steadier than it had been up to the present time. That Sir David Barbour, at the close of his statement, should advocate international bimetallism is very natural, and corresponded with the traditional policy of the Indian Government. The latter, of course, has an exceptionally strong interest in raising the price of silver, and they would like it very well if other countries, with no large silver interests, should help them out of their evil situation. Whether these other nations are seriously injured by experiments in raising the price of silver, is a matter of utter indifference to India.

Meanwhile, a very energetic agitation in favor of the introduction of the gold standard was begun in India in consequence of the Brussels conference and the threatened cessation of silver purchases by the United States. In May 1892, the *Indian Currency Association* was founded, which soon spread over the entire empire. A petition of this organization to the House of Commons, in which they prayed for the substitution of a gold instead of a silver standard, obtained 11,788 signatures, 5289 being Europeans and 6489 being natives. In different places—as in

Kurrachee and Bombay—the first native firms addressed the Government, begging earnestly to be freed from a condition which had become precarious because of the conditions of the currency.

But especially active, as they always were in this question, were the officials of the civil service and the officers. From September 21, 1892, to May 3, 1893, the Government received not less than 1732 addresses from employees who complained of the difficulties caused them by the depreciation of silver; and they were the leaders in the Currency Association.

Very little opposition appears to have arisen in India against the proposed measure, at least it did not produce any such agitation as the efforts of the Currency Association. Only two communications were laid before the Herschell committee which opposed the proposed scheme, one from the Darjeeling and Terai Tea Planters' Association, and another from the United South-Indian Planters' Association. The great mass of the people remained quite passive, chiefly for the reason, probably, that they were completely ignorant of the question.

This time, the efforts aimed at a change of the standard were more successful than formerly. For it was the circles most influential in Indian politics—the Anglo-Indian officials, the cotton manufacturers of Lancashire, chiefly the English firms interested in exporting to India—who resorted to every effort to make the Indian currency independent of the fate of silver. In consequence of the impossibility of making an approximately correct budget, and of the threatened chronic deficits, the condition of the Indian Government, unless the price of silver improved, would be very bad; furthermore, since no one could know what developments would follow the expected cessation of silver purchases by the United States, the British Government assented to the appointment of a commission to investigate the conditions of the Indian currency.

On October 21, 1892, the Secretary of State for India, Earl Kimberley, ordered the appointment of a committee. The Lord High Chancellor, Lord Herschell, was named as chairman;

besides him, the committee consisted of: Mr. Leonard Courtney, M. P.; Sir Thomas Farrer; Sir Reginald Welby, Secretary of the Treasury Office; Mr. Godley, Under-Secretary for India; Lieutenant-General Strachey; and Mr. Currie, member of the India Council.

In his instructions to the chairman, Earl Kimberley especially emphasized the difficult financial condition of the Indian Government. The bases for deliberation were to be communications from the latter on June 21, 1892, and also the correspondence carried on between the India office and the viceroy's Government,—which were laid before the commission. The deliberations were to be secret; and the commission could lay down its own rules of business. The Secretary added that it would be of especial advantage if the report of the commission could be presented before the opening of the Brussels Conference, which is set for November 22, 1892.

But the time was much too short for this; such an exceedingly weighty question could not be solved in a month. The commission held twelve sittings, the first on October 27, 1892, the last on February 22, 1893, at which twenty-seven experts were heard. Attention was also given to a large number of statements which were laid before the committee. On May 31, 1893, the report of the commission, prepared with exceptional care, was laid before the Secretary of State for India. Although the opinions of the experts heard were much divided, the commission unanimously recommended that the Indian mint should be closed to private persons for the free coinage of silver; that the Government should reserve to itself all further coinage of silver rupees; and that the Government treasury should receive gold in payment at a rate of 1s. 4d. for a rupee, thus making the sovereign equal to 15 rupees. The British Government accepted the recommendation of the Herschell committee, and on June 26, 1893, the world was surprised by the decree that the Indian mints were closed to silver.

The stenographic minutes of the "Committee appointed to inquire into the Indian Currency," and the correspondence carried on between the English and Indian Governments, making in all much valuable material, was published and laid before Parliament in a Blue-Book.

What does the measure of June 26, 1893, mean? That the silver rupee, dissevered from the price of silver, has become a credit-coin; and that its maximum worth is fixed at 1s. 4d. If the value of the rupee rises higher than 1s. 4d., it will be advantageous to pay sovereigns into the public treasuries, which are obliged to receive them. If there is a downward movement, the value of the rupee is not fixed.

It is the aim of the measure to make the rate of exchange between England and India independent of the price of silver, and thereby make it steadier; and finally, but only as a secondary object, to prepare the way for the limping gold standard.

In judging the measure it will be well to remember that the history of Holland's currency furnishes us an example of a monetary policy similar to that which India intends to follow. We may perhaps be allowed to digress somewhat more than the mere consideration of Indian affairs properly demands; but as the monetary history of Holland is so exceptionally important and rich in instruction it is to be hoped that this digression will be pardoned.

At the beginning of our century[1] the condition of the Dutch currency was very unsatisfactory. From early times down silver was the chief measure of value, although there prevailed a quite unexampled variety among the silver coins in circulation, due to the fact that, during the existence of the Republic of the United Netherlands, nearly every province had its own coins. Gold coins were likewise struck, their relative values being determined by the Government. But silver was the basis of the currency until 1816. In that year, by the law of September 28, the legal double standard was introduced at a ratio of 1 : 15.87 between the current silver gulden (weighing 200 aas, and 9.61

[1] See Van den Berg, article, "Exchange between Holland and Dutch India" in Palgrave's *Dictionary of Political Economy*, vol i. p. 773, and *Report of the Indian Currency Committee*, § 88.

grams fine) and the ten gulden pieces (containing 6.056 grams fine gold).

Inasmuch as gold, in comparison with the ratio of 1 : 15½ adopted by France in 1803, was overvalued, all the silver coins of full weight were driven out of the country, and gold coins struck according to the law of 1816 and all depreciated and clipped silver coins of an earlier date formed the only circulating medium of the country.

To improve this condition of things a law was passed March 22, 1839, which reduced the weight of fine silver in the gulden from 9.61 to 9.45 grams. Hence the ratio between gold and silver became 1 : 15.60 instead of 1 : 15.87. But since the gold, in comparison with the French ratio, was still overvalued, the clipping of the old coins continued in a very scandalous fashion, so that a premium of from 5 to 7.50 per centum was often paid for pieces of full weight. A thorough-going reform of the coinage could not be postponed; and a general recoinage of all silver money struck before 1839 was ordered by the law of May 22, 1845.

In a few years the old silver coins were withdrawn from circulation to the nominal value of 85 millions gulden and recoined at a loss of about 8 millions gulden. At the same time the question whether the double standard should be retained was hotly discussed in the press; and, after long debates in Parliament, the law of November 26, 1847, was passed[1] which introduced the single silver standard into Holland with a silver gulden, containing 10.945 grams fine metal, as the unit. All the gold coins in the hands of the public were to be withdrawn and demonetized.

In the Dutch East Indies, at the beginning of the century, the conditions of the currency were if possible, even worse than

[1] Errors have crept in in regard to this date with different authors. Van den Berg, *loc. cit.*, p. 773, and Lexis in *Handwörterbuch der Staatswissenschaften*, vol. v. p. 665, give September 26, 1847. Soetbeer, in *Litteraturnachweis über Geld- und Münzwesen*, Berlin, 1892, p. 55, states November 26, 1846, as the day of the passage of the law, while Nasse, in Schönberg's *Handbuch*, i. p. 365, and Haupt, *Histoire Monétaire*, p. 227, mentioned December 26, 1847.

those in the mother country, and the Government itself helped to ruin the monetary system of the colony.

There prevailed an erroneous view that the needs of the natives were too little developed to demand the use of the precious metals as a medium of exchange. "It is to the interest of the good people of that region to extend the circulation of copper money as far as possible."[1] Since, then, the Government effected the great part of its payments in copper-money—the so-called *duit*—which were introduced from Holland in great quantities, with the unavoidable result that all the good money coined earlier was driven out of the country. Silver was still the legal means of payment, and the silver gulden was the unit of account, but the copper coins remained throughout the whole land the only medium of exchange. A general depreciation of the standard was the natural consequence of this condition of things; if anyone had a payment to make in Holland or anywhere else, he must pay a premium of from 25 to 30 per centum.

The colony suffered severely for many years under this condition of the currency. Finally the Government decided that a drastic measure was required to bring the currency into a satisfactory condition. By the act of May 1, 1854, the coinage system of the mother country, as established by the law of November 26, 1847, was introduced into the Dutch East Indies; and since then influential circles have left nothing undone in order that the colony might share in the advantages of a well-ordered monetary system. In a series of years following, large shipments of silver took place from Holland to Java on the account of the Government, and in 1854–60 alone they amounted to 90 millions gulden. Every opportunity was taken to put silver into circulation instead of the copper money; the long-wished-for reform cost the state 20 millions gulden.

Holland and its colonies, therefore, had a pure silver standard. In consequence of other states going over to gold,

[1] Decree of the Governor-General of the Dutch East Indies, June 25, 1818.

Holland, in 1873,[1] suspended the coinage of silver. Silver could not henceforward be brought to the mint; but neither was gold coined, because Parliament had not yet decided upon a gold coinage or the gold standard. A certain amount of silver coins were at that time in circulation; but their value was fixed neither by the market price of silver nor by that of gold. In the years 1873–75 the demand for coins increased. The result was that, while the price of silver as a metal steadily fell in the markets of the world, the Dutch silver coins became dearer as compared with gold. The London rate of exchange which today oscillates between 12.1 and 12.3 gulden per pound sterling, sank to 11.12 gulden.

In 1875, a limping gold standard was introduced on the basis of a ratio of 1 : 12⅝, and the Dutch mint was opened to gold, while the coinage of silver, with the exception of fractional coins, was forbidden; and it remains so today. A considerable quantity of gold was coined, but retained as a reserve in the vaults of the Central Note Bank, and did not enter into the home circulation. Silver gulden, at their nominal value, remain as a legal tender to any amount, and together with the notes of the Netherlands Bank form the home circulation. Neither silver nor paper has an unconditional claim to be converted into gold, although the Netherlands Bank always gives gold for exportation. In 1881 and 1882 the balance of trade was unfavorable to Holland, and the supply of gold in the Bank, which ordinarily amounted to 80 millions gulden dropped to 5 millions gulden. Under these circumstances a law was passed in April 1884 which empowered the Government to allow the Bank to sell 25 millions of silver gulden at the market price whenever the condition of the currency demanded it. No use was made of this power, but confidence was restored by the measure. They are able to maintain intact the necessary gold reserve which at present amounts to £5,000,000.

In Java there is no mint and very little gold. The amount

[1] The closing of the Utrecht mint was provisionally passed on May 21, 1873, and definitively only by the law of December 3, 1873. See Haupt, *loc. cit.*, p. 228.

of currency, according to a computation in the report of the Herschell committee (§ 88) is:

	In Holland	In Java
	£	£
Gold, about	5,200,000	500,000
Silver	11,000,000	2,773,000
Paper	16,000,000	4,250,000

The experiences which Holland has had with its currency since 1873 are very full of instruction for India. It establishes the fact that with a wise monetary policy it is quite possible, with a favorable balance of payments, to keep the quotations of its currency in the markets of the world far above the intrinsic value of the majority of the coins constituting that currency.[1]

But now, to return to the Dutch East Indies, Java alone has all the great advantage of possessing the same monetary system as the mother country, so that unfavorable rates of exchange can be corrected by the shipment of coin. The rates of exchange are therefore remarkably steady, as the following table[2] shows:

RATES FOR BANK BILLS (SIX MONTHS) FROM BATAVIA ON AMSTERDAM.

Year	Maximum	Minimum	Average
1871	100	103¼	101⅝
1875	99¼	102½	100⅞
1880	99¾	101¼	100½
1885	100½	102	101¼
1886	100¼	101¾	101
1887	100¼	102½	101⅜
1888	101⅝	103	102 3/16
1889	100½	102½	101½
1890	99¾	102	100⅞
1891	99¾	101	100⅜

As to the effects of this monetary system on the country, all

[1] Compare also the interesting statements collected concerning the currency of Canada, West India, British Guyana, Brazil, and other states in the Report of the Indian Currency Committee.

[2] Appendix to *Minutes of the Indian Currency Committee*, p. 232.

are not of the same opinion. Van den Berg, formerly President of the Bank of Java, and now President of the Netherlands Bank, said in 1886 that the crisis of that time—which threatened with annihilation the two most important branches of industry in the country, the cultivation of coffee and cane sugar—was mainly due to the introduction of the limping gold standard. In respect to the mother country, he did not at all recommend a return to the silver standard; but yet he warned every Asiatic government against loosening their hold on the use of silver as a money metal, and urgently advised, rather, a courageous assumption of the losses arising from a depreciating standard. Meanwhile the crisis has disappeared.[1] Whether the gold standard was the cause of it is more than doubtful. On the other hand, the difficulty is explained by the general depression then existing, and, as regards sugar, by the competition of beet sugar. Sir David Barbour, in his special statement in the Final Report of the Gold and Silver Commission (p. 147), remarks: "Netherland India, where the gold standard was adopted, has assuredly not gained by the change in comparison with the other Asiatic countries which maintained the silver standard." Furthermore, the Chamber of Commerce of Sourabaya, not very long ago requested the Dutch minister for the colonies to investigate the monetary conditions[2] of Java, where the chamber asserted that the existing currency was very satisfactory. The minister for the colonies, Keuchenius, then said in the first chamber of the States General, on January 31, 1890, that he very much doubted whether the monetary system prevailing in the Dutch East Indies was sound; it had the appearance to him of resting on a fiction, and on this account he approved of the investigation. Keuchenius, however, shortly after left office, ostensibly in consequence of the reception accorded the above declaration. The opponents of an Asiatic gold standard, in fact, admit that the exports of Java have not suffered; but they believe they would have developed to a very much greater extent, especially to the East Asian silver-

[1] Appendix to *Minutes of the Indian Currency Committee*, p. 232.

[2] *Minutes of the Indian Currency Committee*, Questions 1767 *et seq.*

using countries, if they had not been retarded by the conditions of the currency.

But others point to the fact that during the existence of the limping gold standard the welfare of Java has risen exceptionally; that elsewhere the farmer is seldom found in so fortunate a condition as precisely here. This, for example, is the opinion of Mr. Kensington, a high official of the British-India finance ministry who, in a report of September 21, 1892, expressed[1] himself as remarkably well pleased with what he saw in Java.

To return to India. The opinions regarding the experiences of Java, therefore, following from the enactment of the pure silver standard, do not agree; and on this precedent alone India would probably not be induced to abandon the silver standard. Yet a change was allowed to take place in the conditions of the currency because there was scarcely any other feasible way than the cessation of the free coinage of silver.

To be sure, many other recommendations were made, but all —and rightly—were found to be impracticable. Among the earliest was the talk about the adoption of a high seigniorage of perhaps 10 per centum, or of a duty on silver. The former measure would have led to the same disadvantages which are now feared from the cessation of silver coinage. The financial gain would likewise have been quite unimportant; for it is safe to suppose that in case of the adoption of such a mint charge the coinage would have very materially diminished. Against a high import duty on silver, the difficulties of collection and the danger of smuggling are especially to be urged. It is also very questionable whether, by the adoption of a duty on silver, they would accomplish the purpose of raising the rate of the rupee and limiting the importation of silver, since it is not to be overlooked that the price of silver in the world's markets would fall exactly in proportion to the amount of the duty, if the Indian purchaser would not submit to give more. If they should establish a sliding mint charge, or silver duty, it would open the door to the wildest speculation; and as regards the collection of the silver

[1] Appendix to *Report of the Indian Currency Committee*, p. 232.

duty the difficulties of administration would be inordinately increased.

Yet the coinage of a heavier rupee would give even less help; for after a short time—provided that the price of silver should fall—the difficulties would be the same as exist today.

Others again recommended that they should introduce gold as the unit of account, without the coinage of gold, which should be based on a reserve to be kept by the Bank of England in India; others advised the use of a certain amount of gold as a standard for foreign and for wholesale transactions, treating the coins for domestic trade like fractional currency. Further schemes advocated were: the declaration of the rupee as a legal tender in the United Kingdom; the introduction of the gold standard with gold in circulation, fixing the ratio between both metals from time to time according to the condition of the markets for the precious metals; the issue of treasury notes, based on gold, but simply redeemable in rupees at the daily quotation then existing; the striking of coins made of a composite of gold and silver; the adoption both of a silver and of a gold standard which should exist side by side independent of each other; the coinage of gold money, but only of large denominations (perhaps from 5000 to 10,000 rupees), as the legal tender, degrading the rupee to the level of token money—and to base the paper money on gold alone, but redeemable in gold and silver.

That these propositions amounted to nothing, is evident at first glance. For their venturesome quality some of them are particularly grotesque.

It is yet too soon to decide whether the Indian Government has acted rightly in closing its mints to silver; a knowledge of the effects of the measure is needed for that. As I possess no gift of prophecy, I beg that the following statements be treated simply as my personal view, obtained by an unprejudiced examination of the case, and which does not lay the least claim to absolute certainty.

I believe a distinction should be made between Indian and

English interests. It would certainly be a matter of indifference to the great mass of the Indian people what the standard of the country was, since barter yet prevails in almost all the level part of the land. Only as a tax-payer is the Indian interested that the currency should be as good as possible, and thereby the financial condition of the Government be as strong as possible.

But on the other side, the price of silver in the world's markets must fall heavily on account of the cessation of silver coinage, and consequently the national welfare of India would be seriously threatened. For with such an exceptionally large supply of Indian silver, which Mr. Harrison[1] estimates at Rx. 510 millions, or 54.55 millions kilograms, the losses would amount to hundreds of millions of marks. On this it is to be noted that a great part of the silver hoards consist of coined rupees, and that their value is more firmly fixed by the fact that the native parts with his ornaments only with difficulty; only in times of great distress, such as the frightful famine at the close of the seventies, are ornaments brought to the mints (at that time in three years 45 millions rupees). This is true. But who knows how much silver was melted at that time by the dealers in precious metals before they were brought to the mints? And is it not a misfortune of the worst kind if a native forsakes his last anchor of salvation, his ornaments, in the moment of his greatest need? From time immemorial have the largest classes of the population invested their total savings in silver; so that a sudden fall in its value is not to be treated without consideration, as from the English point of view it is likely to be.

It is urged further that, in case the difference between the value of the coined rupee and its silver contents should become too great, counterfeit coins of full weight would be coined. That would certainly be very undesirable; and the counterfeit pieces would very easily enter into circulation, since, as the Report of the Herschell Committee itself admits, the native is influenced much more by the weight of metal in the coin than by its external appearance. To this it is answered that very

[1] Appendix to *Minutes of the Indian Currency Committee*, p. 307.

bulky and costly machinery is required for counterfeiting—in case it should be profitable—and such it would be difficult to obtain. Against this it is to be said that the Indians are famous as exceptionally clever workers in metals, and how could a European police prevent unauthorized coins from being made in a country of nearly 300 millions of inhabitants! It is my opinion that this danger is over-estimated; the experience of Germany with its thalers, and of the Latin Union with its five-franc pieces, permit this conclusion.

The currency reform is probably of most danger to the Indian industries which export to East Asia. Although the exports of India to China, Japan, etc., are only one-half as large as those to the gold-using countries, there are no corresponding imports such as come from Europe, and the Indian balance of trade is kept so strongly favorable only by the trade with East Asia. Now India has a different currency from the countries which form its mainstay. What will be the effect? That the export of opium to China should seriously decline does not appear very likely, for the Indian opium is there a luxury for which something more can be exacted. But how as to the cotton industry? They have now the disadvantage as compared with Lancashire that they do not in the least possess any such organized money market as the English manufacturers have at hand in the London markets, and which is absolutely necessary to enable them to compete. It will probably now become very much easier for the infant cotton industry of China and especially of Japan to again drive the Bombay people from the home market.

That the exports of India to gold-using countries would be injured by the closing of the mints, I do not believe; it is the contrary. To all appearances the rate of exchange will now remain very much steadier than formerly, when it was entirely independent of the condition of the silver market; and that is an invaluable gain to trade. The view that the depreciation of silver served as a premium on exports in Indian trade has now very little value; for we said, in Chapter II., that at least for the exports of Indian grain a favorable effect of the currency was not proved, and that India's exports, as well as its ability to compete in the world's markets, depend far more on other things than on the condition of the exchanges.

In this question the English should be distinguished from the Indian interests; they do not always coincide. But even England's interest depends not so much on a rise as on the stability of the rates of exchange, although a rise would be of great advantage to the United Kingdom.

There are also the firms engaged in exportation to East India. To them it is certainly not important to keep the rates of exchange steady, but if possible to raise the value of the rupee.

That the interests of the European officials in India especially demand a change of the standard, probably no one would claim; a measure such as Ceylon adopted, by fixing the salaries of its officers at 1s. 10½d., would have served the same purpose. This, however, would have the same effect as the adoption of an obligation to pay in gold, because it would have burdened the Indian tax-payer to the same extent. But something must be done, if the integrity of the bureaucracy and therewith the position of England in India is to be preserved.

Finally this plays a chief rôle: it is the interest of England to keep the Indian Government in a strong financial condition so that it may be able to aid in the defense of the British Empire, as it has done to the present time. Since English rule in India undoubtedly means a great gain to civilization, and its maintenance is also highly desirable in the interests of the Indian people, the interests of India and those of England here may partly coincide.

Whether the measure adopted was the right one, it is too soon, as before observed, to decide. But after the closing of the mints the currency policy of the Government does not appear to have been free from error. I do not think it was proper, during the period of the crisis naturally following such a thoroughgoing measure, for the Indian Government to try to continue the sale of council bills at a time when the country's balance of trade —only temporarily, one would hope—became unfavorable. In the end such exceptionally skillful business men as the English may here succeed in finding the right way, since it is a matter of vital importance to their power in the world.

They will surely succeed also in preventing the Indian currency from becoming dangerous to the gold standards of Europe. For should the Indian Government sometime succeed in keeping a permanently stable rate of exchange, in order to prepare for the coming of the limping gold standard,—the mother country would look strictly to see that no scarcity of gold should result—which would be of most serious import to her. In the main I believe that the effect on the gold supplies of the world of finally introducing the limping gold standard into India is overestimated. Gold can always be used as money in India only to a limited extent; it is even claimed that the present silver coins are of too great value for the great mass of the Indian transactions, and that therefore copper coins are mostly in daily use.[1] How then would it be with gold coins?

The English have no sentiment in colonial policies. They will be first of all careful that the currency policy shall not injure them, nor Europe.

[1] Compare Dr. G. Ruhland, "Zwei bimetallistiche Theorien," in the *Frankfurter Zeitung*, Morgenblatt No. 36, February 5, 1894.

APPENDIX I.

MINUTE BY THE HONORABLE SIR DAVID BARBOUR,[1] K. C. S. I.

1. In dealing with the currency of British India it is necessary to draw a distinction between the active rupee circulation and the total number of rupees in existence. A large proportion of the rupees issued from the mints and not melted down are kept as permanent hoards and fulfill none of the functions of money. This distinction cannot, however, be sharply drawn, as rupees are always liable to pass from hoards into the active circulation, and *vice versa*. What I call the active rupee circulation may be held to include all the rupees which at some period of each year are used as money.

The total active rupee circulation has recently been estimated at Rx. 115,000,000.

Without accepting these figures as more than an approximation to the truth, they are sufficient to show that a gold standard with a purely gold currency is impossible in India. To establish a gold currency in India with a full legal tender currency composed entirely of gold, it would be necessary to withdraw from circulation about 1,150 millions of rupees, to melt them down, and sell them for what they would fetch as silver bullion, and then to replace them by about £77,000,000 worth of gold.

In the present conditions of India and of the silver and gold markets this would be an impossible operation.

Moreover, a gold standard with a purely gold currency of full legal tender coins would not suit India (even if it were possible to introduce it), because the gold coins would in practice be of too great value to suit the vast majority of Indian transactions.

2. It follows from what has been stated in the preceding paragraph that if we are to have a gold standard in India, a large proportion of the circulation must consist of silver coins, and these coins must be a legal tender to any amount. The example of France and other countries shows that it is possible to have a gold standard, although a large per-

[1] Appendix I., *Minutes of the Indian Currency Committee*, p. 147.

centage of the circulation consists of overvalued silver coins which are legal tender to any amount.

In order that the gold standard may be effective, a limit must, however, be placed to the number of such coins, and they must be convertible into gold coins, either without payment of premium or on payment of a trifling premium, whenever any person wishes for gold coins in exchange for silver coins.

So long as the silver coins are freely exchangeable for gold coins in accordance with their face values, the gold standard is effectively maintained.

3. I have no doubt that even with a gold standard the people of India would in almost all their transactions prefer to employ silver rupees. It is improbable that a gold coin of less than Rs. 10 in value would be issued in India, and such a coin would be quite unsuited for ordinary Indian transactions. Rs. 10 represents, generally, much more than a cooly's wages for a month, and if a cooly received his wages in the form of a single coin he would immediately exchange it for smaller coins. We could not pay our soldiers or police in gold coins. Payments to the opium cultivators could not be made in gold; neither could the ryots pay their rents in gold.

There would also be a not unreasonable dread among the common people that gold coins might be of light weight; they would generally be unwilling to accept them, and for monetary purposes in ordinary life gold coins would hardly be used. This would be the case, I believe, even if gold coins of the value of only Rs. 5 each were issued.

4. It may, then, be taken for granted that with a gold standard the great bulk of the Indian currency must continue to be silver rupees, and that for monetary purposes there would ordinarily be no considerable demand for gold coins in exchange for silver. On the contrary the demand for monetary purposes would rather be for silver coins in exchange for gold coins. Gold coins would only, as a rule, be required in exchange for silver coins, when gold was required for hoarding, for export, or to be melted down for ornaments.

It follows that with a gold standard India would require, and would use, a very large amount of silver rupees, and would neither require nor use a large number of gold coins.

Any gold coins that were put into circulation, and were not melted down or hoarded, would very quickly find their way into the hands of bankers and dealers in bullion, into the government treasuries and into the Paper Currency Reserve.

5. For the purpose of introducing a gold standard into India, we might stop the free coinage of silver, adopt measures for accumulating a store of gold, and, when what was considered a sufficient stock of gold had been obtained, we might open the mints to the free coinage of gold, make gold coins a legal tender and guarantee by means of our accumulated stock of gold the exchangeability of silver for gold coins according to their face values. I do not recommend this plan; the accumulation of a sufficient store of gold would be a measure too expensive for a country situated as India is, and when it had been accumulated and the exchangeability of the silver coins for gold coins had been guaranteed by means of it, there would be a very great risk of the whole stock of gold being drawn away in exchange for silver rupees. If this should happen, and I think it would happen unless our stock of gold was very large indeed, the gold standard would cease to exist, and we should find ourselves exactly where we started.

6. The only measures for the introduction of a gold standard into India which seem to me feasible are the following:

(1) The first measure would be the stoppage of the free coinage of silver. Government would retain the right of purchasing silver and coining it into rupees.

(2) The next measure would be to open the mints to the free coinage of gold. Any man bringing gold to the mints would be entitled to have it coined into gold coins, which would be legal tender to any amount. It would be desirable to stop the free coinage of silver some time before opening the mints to the free coinage of gold. It would be a valuable guide to us in subsequent proceedings to know exactly what effect the stoppage of the free coinage of silver had on the gold value of the rupee.

The new gold coins might be a 10-rupee piece and a 20-rupee piece.

7. The weight and fineness of the gold coins to be issued from the mint would be such that the par of exchange between them and the sovereign would be the exchange which it was desired to establish between India and England.

For example, if we wished the rupee to be worth 1s. 4d. the 10-rupee coin would contain as much gold as was worth (1s. 4d.) $\times$ 10 = 160 pence.

The quantity of fine gold in the 10-rupee piece would be $\frac{160}{240}$, or two-thirds of the quantity contained in the sovereign.

8. The question of the ratio at which we should change from the silver to the gold standard would require careful consideration.

We ought not to think of going back to the old ratio of 1 : 15½. Neither ought we to adopt the very lowest price to which silver may have fallen at any time, or to consider ourselves bound to accept the market ratio of the very moment at which the change was made. A ratio based on the average price of silver during a limited period before the introduction of the gold standard would probably be both the safest and the most equitable.

9. We may be quite sure that, on the introduction of the gold standard, bankers and bullion dealers away from the Presidency towns and, perhaps, in the Presidency towns, would charge something for changing silver coins for gold ones. The general public, however, would very seldom require to make such exchanges, and, if all Government Treasuries were required to give gold coins for silver coins whenever it was possible for them to do so, there could not be any considerable premium on gold coins so long as there were such coins in the public Treasuries or in the Paper Currency Reserve, and the gold standard would, subject to the above condition, be effectively maintained.

10. After the above measures had been carried out, it might happen that no gold was brought to the Mints to be coined and put into circulation, and that the rupee fell in value below 1s. 4d.

Or, it might happen that though gold was brought to the mints for a time and the rupee was worth 1s. 4d., yet subsequently gold ceased to be brought to the Mints, the gold coins disappeared from circulation, and the rupee fell below 1s. 4d.

If gold were not brought to the Mint to be coined and put into circulation, or if gold coins disappeared and gold ceased to be brought to the Mints, it would be a sign that the rupee currency was redundant, or, in other words, that there were too many silver rupees in circulation, that consequently their value had fallen below 1s. 4d. each, that gold coins had been driven out of circulation, and that the gold standard was no longer effectively maintained.

The remedy in such case would be to contract the rupee currency, and to adopt any feasible measures for improving the general financial position of the country. An improvement in the general financial position would give increased confidence, and the reduction of the rupee currency, if carried far enough, must ultimately restore the value of that coin.

11. The greatest danger from the cause just indicated would arise immediately after the first introduction of the gold standard, and would be brought about by silver rupees being returned into India from foreign countries, and by their being thrown into active circulation from Indian hoards. I think that Indian rupees would certainly be returned to India from abroad when their value in India became greater than their bullion value, but I now doubt very much if Indian rupees would be largely brought out of hoards. It is more likely that existing hoards of rupees would practically remain unaffected. I formerly held a different opinion on this point, and believed that rupees would be largely brought out of hoards when they were given a value exceeding that of the metal contained in them.

12. The reduction of the rupee currency in the manner just indicated, if it became necessary, might or might not prove a very expensive measure. It could, of course, be spread over a number of years, but until it had been carried out to a sufficient extent the gold standard would not be effectively maintained. When the rupee currency had once been sufficiently reduced I should not expect any serious difficulty in the future.

Looking to the increase of population in India, to the rapid opening out of the country, and to the comparatively small part which credit plays in Indian trade, it may fairly be held that even with a gold standard an increase of the rupee currency would be required every year, and that increase I place at not less than Rx. 1,000,000 yearly. It might be considerably more, twice or three times as much. When the coinage of rupees was stopped, any redundancy of the silver currency would be diminished yearly by this amount without any action on our part. It is also not impossible that rupees would continue to be withdrawn from the active circulation to be hoarded as at present; they would certainly be hoarded by persons whose savings were small. This cause would still further reduce any temporary redundancy of the silver currency at first starting. Of course while the reduction of the rupee currency was in progress we would not have an effective gold standard, but even during that period of uncertainty I should expect the exchange with England to remain much steadier than it has been during the last few years. It would cease to be blown up and down by every breath of speculation, and, if we could establish confidence in our measures, the rate of exchange would tend strongly towards the rate we had decided to maintain, and would only diverge from it under the pressure of real economic forces.

A nation that possessed a fairly satisfactory standard of value might well hesitate to expose itself even temporarily to the evils of an inconvertible standard, but no such argument applies in the case of India. We already labor under difficulties which are quite as great as those to which an inconvertible paper standard would expose us. The prospect of being unable for a time to effectively establish the gold standard need not, therefore, deter us from the attempt to do so if we see a prospect of success in the future.

13. It is also possible that under certain conditions of trade there might be more gold brought to the Mint and put into circulation than was required for ordinary use as currency.

In that case the public would get rid of the gold coins by paying them into the Government Treasuries. Gold might accumulate in these Treasuries, and the Government could not in practice relieve the Treasuries by forcing gold coins on persons who preferred to receive payment in silver.

The proper remedy for any such accumulation of gold would be for the Treasuries to pass the gold coins into the Paper Currency Reserve, which could absorb several millions without difficulty, and the Paper Currency Reserve could be relieved, when necessary, by remitting the gold to England in payment of debts, its place being taken by silver rupees.

No serious difficulty arising from an over-supply of gold coins need, therefore, be feared.

14. It is important to consider what the additional demand for gold would be, owing to the establishment of a gold standard in India.

Taking the active circulation at Rx. 115,000,000, I think that gold coins to the value of one-fifth of that amount would be an ample proportion of the active circulation for the purpose of maintaining the gold standard. This would be Rx. 23,000,000 worth of gold, or, say, 15,000,0000 pounds sterling. I believe that the gold standard would be maintained effectively with a smaller amount of gold, and that gold in excess of £15,000,000 in the active circulation would be unnecessary and might be a source of positive inconvenience. When we had arrived at normal conditions the yearly additions of gold required for the active currency would be small, and would probably not exceed £200,000 yearly.

15. It is more than probable, however, that the substitution of a gold standard for a silver standard would lead to the increased use of gold instead of silver for hoarding. On the question of the extent to which this substitution of gold for silver would ultimately be carried, I am unable to offer any opinion.

Silver is at present used for hoarding (as a store of value), and for ornament. When it ceased to be the monetary standard of India it would be less suitable for hoarding, but it might continue to be largely hoarded in the form of rupees, and, on the other hand, silver bullion would fall considerably in value and price, and its greater cheapness would tend to increase its use for purposes of ornament. It must be uncertain to what extent gold would begin to take the place of silver for hoarding and ornaments after the establishment of a gold standard, but in the first instance, at any rate, the extent of the change would probably not be considerable.

It is held by some that, if a gold standard were established in India, a great deal of the gold that is now hoarded or held in the form of ornaments would be brought to the Mints, coined, and put into circulation. I have never been able to accept this theory. Why should a native of India give up his habit of hoarding, or an Indian lady cease to take a pleasure in the wearing or possession of gold ornaments, merely because the Government of India had established a gold standard?

There is, however, a large amount of gold imported into this country every year, and there must always be a considerable amount of gold in the hands of bullion dealers. I think that if we had an effective gold standard it is very likely that all this gold, which is, as it were waiting till the time of absorption arrives, would be coined and become part of the circulation for the time. To facilitate this result, I would propose not to charge any seigniorage on gold coins.

16. In this paper I have dealt with the question of a gold standard for India from a practical point of view. Many objections, founded on considerations not of an immediately practical nature, may be raised to the introduction of a gold standard into India. Some of these objections appear to me to possess weight; others I believe to be imaginary. I have no hesitation in saying that an international agreement for the free coinage of both silver and gold, and for the making of them full legal tender at a fixed ratio, would be far better for India

and all other countries than the establishment of the single gold standard, even if the latter course be possible.

Under the former system the worst result that could happen would be the disappearance of one of the metals from circulation, but this would only happen by the other metal taking its place and gradually driving it out, and under such circumstances all countries would have the same standard.

The general adoption of the system of double legal tender would be a perfectly safe measure, and would be a final settlement of the question. The attempt to establish a general gold standard is not free from risk. History affords instances of the establishment of a gold standard in one or more countries, but sooner or later the standard was changed. It may, however, be that the conditions of gold mining have so greatly changed that a gold standard can now be maintained for an indefinite period.

17. With regard to the question of the expediency of attempting to introduce a gold standard into India, I do not go further than saying that, if a general agreement for the free coinage of both silver and gold at a ratio cannot be obtained, and if the United States does not adopt free coinage of silver, I think an attempt should be made to establish a gold standard in this country.

I believe that a perpetuation of the difference of monetary standards between England and her Indian Empire would be a source of incalculable mischief to both England and India, and that such a state of things should not be accepted until it has been proved by actual experiment to be absolutely unavoidable.

June 21, 1892.

APPENDIX II.

IMPORTS AND EXPORTS OF MERCHANDISE; IMPORTS AND EXPORTS OF GOLD; VALUE OF GOLD COINED; IMPORTS AND EXPORTS OF SILVER; VALUE OF SILVER COINED; RECEIPTS FROM SALE OF BILLS AND CABLE TRANSFERS ON THE INDIAN GOVERNMENT; AVERAGE PAPER CIRCULATION.

[Taken from the *Third Report of the Royal Commission on the Depression of Trade and Industry*, pp. 385 *et seq.*; from Appendix XII. at the end of the *Report of the Gold and Silver Commission* (*appendix to final report*, p. 112); and from the *Appendix to the Report of the Indian Currency Committee*, p. 240.]

Fiscal Year	Average Rate of Exchange		Imports of Merchandise, exclusive of Precious Metals	Exports of Merchandise, exclusive of Precious Metals	Excess of Imports of Mdse. exclusive of Precious Metals	Imports of Gold	Exports of Gold	Excess of Imports of Gold	Value of Gold Coined	Imports of Silver	Exports of Silver	Excess of Imports of Silver	Value of newly coined Silver, exclusive of recoinage	Receipts from Sale of Bills and Cable Transfers on the Indian Governm't	Paper Money Circulation
	s.	d.	in 1000 Rx.	in 1000 Rx.	in 1000 Rx.	in 1000 Rx.	in 1000 Rx.	in 1000 Rx.	in 1000 Rx.	in 1000 Rx.	in 1000 Rx.	in 1000 Rx.	in 1000 Rx.	in 1000 £	
1835-36 — 1839-40 Yearly average	1	11.100	5,285	11,645	6,361	343	10	333	69	2,097	254	1,843	3,323	1,916	No circulation of state paper money before 1862.
1840-41 — 1844-45 Yearly average	1	10.850	8,676	14,935	6,259	329	2	326	25	3,159	688	2,472	3,762	2,056	
1845-46 — 1849-50 Yearly average	1	10.000	9,045	15,819	6,774	1,003	24	979	47	1,870	1,276	593	2,707	2,506	
1850-51 — 1854-55 Yearly average	1	11.900	11,547	19,346	7,799	1,159	82	1,077	67	3,155	971	2,185	3,797	3,371	
1855-56	2	0.125	13,943	23,038	9,095	2,508	2	2,506	168	8,793	598	8,194	6,974	1,484	
1856-57	2	1.125	14,194	25,338	11,144	2,176	85	2,091	128	12,238	1,164	11,073	10,779	2,820	
1857-58	2	0.625	15,278	27,456	12,178	2,830	47	2,783	44	12,985	766	12,219	12,551	629	
1858-59	Sepoy		21,729	29,863	8,134	4,437	10	4,426	132	8,380	651	7,728	6,518	26	
1859-60	Rebellion		24,265	27,960	3,695	4,288	4	4,284	64	12,069	921	11,148	10,677	5	
1855-56 — 1859-60 Yearly average	2	0.325	17,882	26,731	8,849	3,248	30	3,218	107	10,893	820	10,072	9,500	993	—
1860-61	—		23,494	32,971	9,477	4,242	10	4,233	65	6,435	1,107	5,328	5,192	0.8	—
1861-62	1	11.867	22,320	36,317	13,997	5,190	6	5,184	59	9,762	675	9,086	7,070	1,194	—
1862-63	1	11.920	22,632	47,860	25,227	6,882	33	6,848	131	13,627	1,077	12,550	9,251	6,642	4,419
1863-64	1	11.907	27,146	65,625	38,480	8,925	27	8,898	54	14,037	1,240	12,797	11,480	8,980	5,233
1864-65	1	11.876	28,151	68,027	39,876	9,875	35	9,840	96	11,488	1,410	10,079	10,486	6,789	6,882
1860-61 — 1864-65 Yearly average	1	11.892	24,749	50,160	25,411	7,023	22	7,001	81	11,070	1,102	9,968	8,696	4,721	5,511
1865-66	1	11.835	29,599	65,491	35,892	6,373	648	5,724	18	20,184	1,516	18,669	14,507	6,966	7,726
1866-67	1	11.064	29,039	41,860	12,821	4,581	739	3,842	28	8,655	1,692	6,963	6,119	5,068	8,989
1867-68	1	11.190	35,706	50,874	15,168	4,776	166	4,609	22	6,999	1,405	5,594	4,313	4,137	9,285
1868-69	1	11.197	36,990	53,062	17,072	5,177	18	5,159	25	9,979	1,378	8,601	4,207	3,706	10,146
1869-70	1	11.267	32,928	52,471	19,544	5,690	98	5,592	79	8,264	944	7,320	7,474	6,980	10,669

Fiscal Year	Average Rate of Exchange	Imports of Merchandise, exclusive of Precious Metals	Exports of Merchandise, exclusive of Precious Metals	Excess of Imports of Mdse. exclusive of Precious Metals	Imports of Gold	Exports of Gold	Excess of Imports of Gold	Value of Gold Coined	Imports of Silver	Exports of Silver	Excess of Imports of Silver	Value of newly coined Silver, exclusive of recoinage	Receipts from Sale of Bills and Cable Transfers on the Indian Governm't	Paper Money Circulation
	s. d.	in 1000 Rx.	in 1000 Rx.	in 1000 Rx.	in 1000 Rx.	in 1000 Rx.	in 1000 Rx.	in 1000 Rx.	in 1000 Rx.	in 1000 Rx.	in 1000 Rx.	in 1000 Rx.	in 1000 £	
1865–66 — 1869–70 Yearly average	1 11.310	32,652	52,752	20,099	5,320	334	4,986	34	10,817	1,387	9,429	7,324	5,371	9,363
1870–71	1 10.495	34,469	55,331	20,863	2,783	500	2,282	4	2,662	1,720	942	1,718	8,444	9,813
1871–72	1 11.126	32,092	63,186	31,094	3,574	8	3,565	15	8,000	1,468	6,532	1,690	10,310	11,416
1872–73	1 10.754	31,875	55,251	23,376	2,622	79	2,543	32	1,913	1,219	715	3,981	13,939	12,864
1873–74	1 10.351	33,836	54,996	21,160	1,649	266	1,383	15	4,144	1,648	2,496	2,370	13,286	11,145
1874–75	1 10.356	36,222	56,359	20,137	2,089	216	1,874	14	6,052	1,410	4,642	4,897	10,842	10,650
1870–71 — 1874–75 Yearly average	1 10.576	33,699	57,025	23,326	2,543	214	2,329	16	4,558	1,493	3,065	2,931	11,364	11,178
1875–76	1 9.625	38,887	58,091	19,204	1,836	291	1,545	17	3,464	1,909	1,555	2,550	12,390	11,352
1876–77	1 8.508	37,441	61,014	23,573	1,444	1,236	207	—	9,992	2,794	7,198	6,271	12,696	11,642
1877–78	1 8.791	41,464	65,222	23,758	1,579	1,111	468	16	15,777	1,100	14,676	16,180	10,134	13,250
1878–79	1 7.794	37,801	60,938	23,137	1,463	2,359	—986	—	5,594	1,623	3,971	7,211	13,949	13,291
1879–80	1 7.961	41,166	67,212	26,046	2,050	300	1,751	15	9,605	1,735	7,870	10,257	15,263	12,798
1875–76 — 1879–80 Yearly average	1 8.534	39,352	62,496	23,144	1,674	1,060	615	10	8,886	1,832	7,054	8,494	12,886	12,447
1880–81	1 7.956	53,117	74,581	21,464	3,672	17	3,655	13	5,316	1,424	3,893	4,250	15,240	13,063
1881–82	1 7.895	49,113	81,968	32,855	4,856	12	4,844	34	6,466	1,087	5,379	2,188	18,412	13,505
1882–83	1 7.525	52,096	83,485	31,389	5,095	164	4,931	17	8,358	878	7,480	6,506	15,121	15,181
1883–84	1 7.536	55,279	88,176	22,896	5,469	7	5,463	—	7,409	1,002	6,406	3,663	17,600	13,387
1884–85	1 7.308	55,703	83,255	27,552	4,778	106	4,671	13	9,110	1,864	7,245	5,794	13,759	14,541
1880–81 — 1884–85 Yearly average	1 7.644	53,062	82,293	29,231	4,774	61	4,712	16	7,332	1,251	6,081	4,480	16,026	13,935
1885–86	1 6.254	55,656	83,881	28,225	3,092	329	2,763	23	12,386	780	11,607	10,286	10,293	14,710
1886–87	1 5.441	61,777	88,470	26,693	2,834	656	2,177	—	8,220	1,064	7,156	4,617	12,136	14,201
1887–88	1 4.898	65,005	90,544	25,539	3,136	244	2,992	—	10,590	1,361	9,229	10,788	15,359	16,162
1888–89	1 4.379	69,440	97,050	27,609	3,119	305	2,814	23	10,726	1,479	9,247	7,282	14,263	16,432
1889–90	1 4.566	69,197	103,460	34,263	5,071	456	4,615	23	12,388	1,451	10,938	8,551	15,474	16,151
1885–86 — 1889–90 Yearly average	1 5.107	64,215	92,681	28,466	3,470	398	3,072	14	10,862	1,227	9,635	8,311	13,505	15,531
1890–91	1 6.090	71,975	100,227	28,252	6,501	865	5,636	—	15,444	1,259	14,175	13,163	15,969	22,889
1891–92	1 4.733	69,432	108,174	38,741	4,119	1,705	2,414	25	10,604	1,582	9,022	5,554	16,401	25,436
1892–93	1 2.985	66,279	106,575	40,296	1,782	4,594	–2,813	?	15,228	2,364	12,864	12,705	16,225	26,402

EXPORTS OF WHEAT FROM INDIA AND THE RATES OF EXCHANGE.[1]

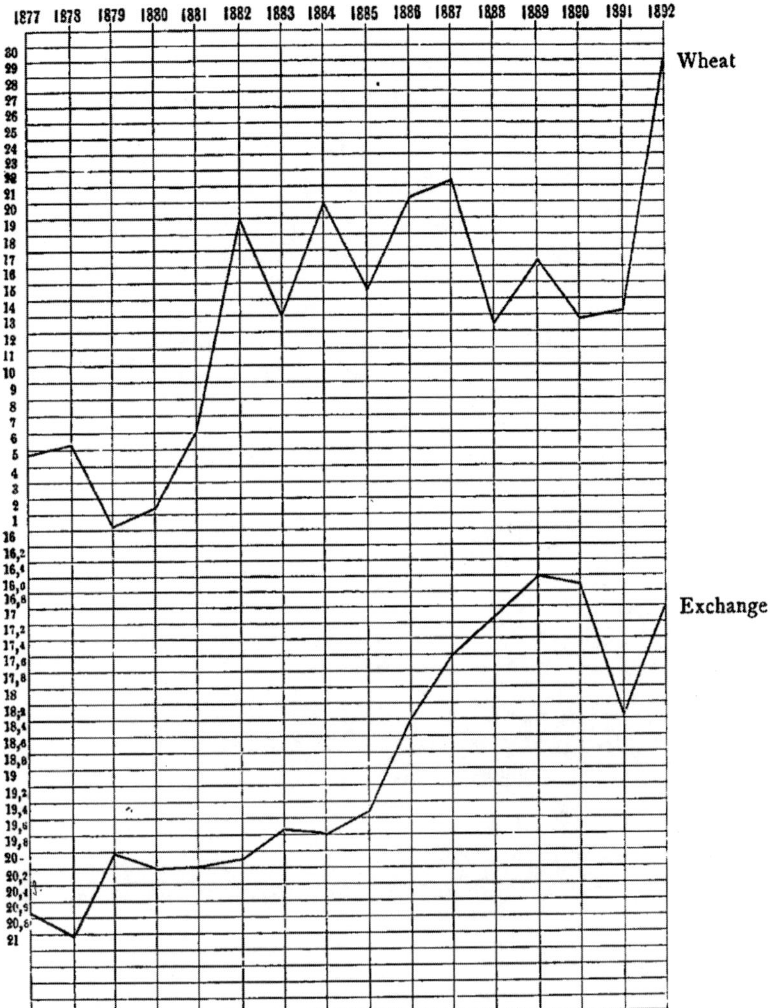

[1] The figures in the scale represent millions of cwts. for wheat; and, in the scale for the exchanges, the figures give the number of pence to the rupee.